A **WESTERN HORSEMAN**®

CW00547671

RANCH-HORSE VERSATILITY

A Winner's Guide to Successful Rides

By Mike Major With Fran Devereux Smith

Edited by
Fran Devereux Smith and Cathy Martindale

Photography by
John Brasseaux
Darrell Dodds
Ross Hecox
Jim Jennings/Courtesy *The American Quarter Horse Journal*
Jeff Kirkbride Photography

Illustrations by Ron Bonge

Ranch-Horse Versatility

Published by
WESTERN HORSEMAN magazine
2112 Montgomery St.
Fort Worth, TX 76107
817-737-6397

www.westernhorseman.com

Design, Typography and Production
Globe Pequot Press
Guilford, Connecticut

Front Cover Photo by **John Brasseaux**
Back Cover Photo by **Darrell Dodds**

Printing
Versa Press, Inc.
East Peoria, Illinois

Printed in the United States of America

First Printing: May 2011

ISBN 978-0-7627-7335-0

DEDICATION AND ACKNOWLEDGMENTS

I want to dedicate this book to God first because if it wasn't for God giving me the ability and drive to learn about horses, where would I be? I'd be nothing. Some people call it luck or whatever, but I feel like God's blessings poured out to me are all the championships we've won with our horses. Without saying that, I can't take much credit for those titles.

I have to recognize my dad for giving me all those opportunities to ride horses—every kind of horse experience, from running racehorses to breaking colts—and he always saw that we kids had plenty of cattle to work on all the ranches we ran. From the time I was little, Dad tried to get me to read a cow and figure out what she was thinking. "Look at that cow," he'd say. "You ought to be able to tell what she's thinking, what she's going to do."

He always made us open our minds to think about such things, and that fell right in with handling the horses, too. "Can you control your horse and figure out what he's thinking?" he'd ask. For that way of approaching stock and all the opportunities and all the horses to ride, I have to thank my dad.

Of course, I also have to thank Bob Lee. He showed me an entirely different side to horses than I had ever seen before, as far as cutting horses and their responsiveness goes.

To my wife, Holly, I have to say thanks for the showmanship part of this versatility ranch-horse competition. I couldn't have done these things without her and all the work she's done with 4-H and showing. All that gave her so much insight on horsemanship, and she's helped me learn to be particular and to be right on the spot when I compete. Holly went to the world in judging, and when I come out of the arena, she's never been afraid to tell me that I was off here or there in showing my horse. She isn't being mean; she just tells me when I don't look so good. And if somebody's not telling the truth, they aren't helping at all. So thanks, Holly, for the help.

This book also is dedicated to the horses I've ridden. They have taught me more than anything or anybody else could teach me. Horses are the best teachers, and the tougher the horse, the more he can teach me. If I'm not riding, I'm not listening, and I'm not learning from the horses.

All the horsemen I've known in my life, all the ropers and the cowboys, have inspired me to be a better horseman, and I'm very grateful for that. They've made me think about what I needed to do to get my horses to ride like theirs. Some of those horsemen don't even know they've been such great inspirations to me, but I appreciate them all the same.

Mike Major

CONTENTS

FOREWORD

The first time I ever saw Mike Major, he was riding a really nice bay gelding, a heading horse, and Mike could sure-enough rope on him. Then I started talking to Mike, and we became good friends. We've lived here in the same area for a long time now. I've watched Mike ride horses through the years, and he's come a long way with his horsemanship. He's really tough in the arena, too.

I've thought and thought about what to say about this man. Golly, Mike can build a house; he can build a barn; he can weld, make spurs and bits. This son-of-a-gun can even dance more than just a little, and hauls his own cattle in his own trucks. Anything he wants to do, he can do. He's amazing.

Plus, this man is a cowboy. He's not just a little cowboy; he's a lot cowboy, and he is a horseman. He knows what a horse is supposed to look like. Everything he does with a horse is right. It's correct, and he makes some really nice horses. A lot of people wear a hat and a pair of boots and spurs, and they can't even pack Mike's doggone bridle.

Mike's not just a reiner or just a roper. He's a hand with horses, who can put that simple little one-step, two-step lead change on a horse. When Mike takes a horse somewhere, he can do a little bit of everything. I admire the way Mike rides his horses and treats them.

Out in the pasture is where it all begins with a young horse. That's real, and that's where Mike starts with his horses. That's why they're broke and anybody can do about anything he wants to do on one. That was my deal years ago and the way I made my horses—I did everything on them. Today it's hard to find somebody who does that, and it takes a man like Mike with his horses to bring the Quarter Horse back to what it should be. It's great that people are interested in the ranch-horse versatility because we've about lost those horses that do everything and don't wear out. And that might be because people don't want to work as hard as Mike works with a horse.

Something else about Mike that I think is great: You don't hear Mike blowing any

Sunny Jim Orr, seen here with wife Rayann, has trained and shown many outstanding horses. As a judge, he was the first to make Zan Parr Bar grand champion—as a yearling, back when a young colt received no points for that. "People looked down their noses a little at me for doing that, " said Orr, "but a little later, I looked like I was really smart."

Orr's horse savvy also prompted him to show Diamond Sparkle at halter, start riding her, make her an AQHA Champion, and then win the Super Horse title on her. "That mare was a good one," he said, and added with a grin, "Then Carol (Rose) bought her and made her famous."

smoke. You don't hear him bragging about his horses, but his horses will beat you. Every time I see Mike on that black mare he's showing now, I tell him how nice she is, and he always says she's coming along pretty good. He says a horse is nice, but doesn't do a lot of bragging. Then he takes Smart Whiskey Doc or that mare to a show, and at the end of the class, he's packing off the blue ribbon.

What makes Mike's horses so good is that he does things with them, and he cowboys with them, and he's a horseman. That's all there is to it. There are few like him today. Most horses like that young black mare will last a long time, and that all goes back to Mike's way of doing things.

Today, for instance, Mike's riding young horses, so he's using nice, slow roping steers for his heading horses and giving those colts a chance to think. He handles every colt a little and teaches that horse how to use himself to do things. That's Mike using his noggin.

Mike's probably the only man around today that I'd let ride one of my colts. I've raised four lately out of a double-bred Two Eyed Jack mare and by a son of Docs JJay, by Doc Bar. I'm 75 now and people asked last spring if I was going to start my 2-year-old. I told 'em, "Yep, but if I get in trouble, I'm going to see Major." I've gotten along all right, but I knew that if I got in trouble, Mike was there.

I'm roping on the 3- and 4-year-olds, and my wife's riding the 5-year-old. We're horseback, and that's my retirement. I can go out the back door, saddle my horses and rope—just like I want to. That's all I know—saddle a horse and go ride, and I've been fortunate and had some nice horses to ride in my life. I figure if I can ride and come down here to Mike's and rope with these kids once in a while, I couldn't ask for a better retirement.

I'm pretty high on Mike Major—as a man and as a friend. The only thing I know to say about Mike is just what Mike is. There's no putting any polish on it, no blowing him up, no deal of making him 10 times bigger than he is. He's a horseman and he's a cowboy. I hold the man in very high regard.

Sunny Jim Orr
Pueblo, Colorado

INTRODUCTION

Ranch horses long have been hard-working laborers in the American livestock industry, doing their jobs no matter the weather, terrain or circumstance. Now these horses have come into their own in the competitive arena, vying for top honors as a show's most versatile ranch horse.

Developing a responsive, multipurpose ranch horse always has been the working cowboy's goal. Such a horse is savvy enough to sort a cow from the herd, catch and turn a steer, cover miles of trail, deal with obstacles and complete advanced performance maneuvers—and do so willingly. Now the ranch horse has become the ride of choice for many recreational riders participating in such traditional activities as team roping, reining, and trail riding, as well as versatility events.

A Multipurpose Horse Program

Who better than Mike Major of Fowler, Colo., to discuss the versatile ranch horse and the event that showcases his talents? With his stallion, Smart Whiskey Doc, Mike claimed the American Quarter Horse Association's 2006 Bayer Select Working Cow Horse World Champion title, and "Whiskey" was named World's Greatest Versatility Horse at the National Versatility Ranch Horse Association 2008 and 2009 National Finals. Mike has since ridden Whiskey to two more AQHA national titles, 2009 and 2010 Versatility Ranch Horse Open World Champion.

Ranch-raised in New Mexico, Mike grew up working cattle and riding everything from racehorses, saddle broncs and bucking bulls to cutting and roping horses. He and wife Holly now own and operate Major Cattle Company on the Flying A Ranch, once owned by rodeo company partners Gene Autry and Harry Knight.

Mike and Holly also raise Quarter Horses that multitask on the ranch and in the show arena. Their dual-purpose ranch horses benefit from the fine-tuning necessary for the competitive arena, and their top-flight show horses benefit from ranch work.

"My horses have jobs other than those in the arena, and that's an advantage," Mike admits. "When a horse is a little tired of the show pen, I take him out to gather cattle all morning and brand calves all afternoon. Instead of drilling on him in the arena and making him dread it, I give him a job. It makes all the difference in the world."

A Natural Progression

A few years back, as a result of his success in developing versatile ranch horses, Mike was asked to conduct clinics for versatility enthusiasts and since has gained a following among working cowboys and recreational riders alike. He teaches the hands-on practical application of what he's learned from a lifetime of handling horses and cattle. That's part of the Major family tradition.

"My granddad started it all in the late 1920s and '30s with those remount horses," Mike explains. "When I was growing up, we had nine ranches in New Mexico. My dad traded a lot of cattle and had two feedlots. He believed in his kids working. There were three of us boys, and my three sisters all were as good cowboys as we boys were. We all rode every day—didn't matter if the wind was blowing 70 miles an hour or if it was 20 below zero. We had cattle to work.

"My mom cowboyed as hard as the rest of us. She and I were working cattle one day when my horse bucked off a mountain with me. Later, she told my dad he had to do something; that horse was going to kill me, and I was the only help she had right then. At the time, my brothers and sisters were in public school, but I was home-schooled."

Mike first rode cutting horses as a teen, and he, his brothers and sisters competed successfully in junior rodeos. Their father, Buddy, competed successfully against top professional calf ropers, and Mike always has team-roped competitively.

His father's interest in running stock included Quarter Horses, Thoroughbreds and racing mules. Mike conditioned horses, then rode in matched races until, at age 13, he became too big to be a jockey. At one point, Mike daily rode a racing mule from the ranch headquarters 15 miles to the horse ranch, 2 miles from town, where his brothers and sisters picked him up for school. Each evening,

Holly and Mike Major, and daughters Shanae and Kiana, are shown at the Major Cattle Company headquarters near Fowler, Colorado.

his horses. They turned around and stopped, and he never picked up the bridle reins. That impressed me so much. He was my mentor and still is. He was a built-in part of the horse. Now people at clinics say I look like part of the horse, and I always tell them I owe that to Bob Lee. I was so fortunate to have the opportunity to ride with him."

As for the horse that bucked off the mountain with Mike, Lee made a winning cutting horse of him, and Mike showed him, too. "That big, ugly rawboned Thoroughbred just melted in front of a cow," Mike says, "and I hand that all to Bob. But the horse never quit bucking."

Building the Bloodlines

As a young man, Mike rode for the public and wanted his own horse operation. Two of his father's fillies would make a nice start for a broodmare band, but Buddy Major had no intention of selling the mares outright to Mike. Instead, Mike had to break and ride five of his father's mules.

Mike purchased a black stallion with Leo and Three Chicks bloodlines, and in the early 1980s started his New Mexico horse operation in Vequita. A Mito Bars- and Sugar Bars-bred stallion followed, and in 1989 Joys Double Feature joined the stallion line-up. "Smokey," as the gray was known, had Beduino, Rebel Cause and Truckle Feature breeding, and became a top roping and cow horse. As always, Mike team-roped competitively and also entered ranch rodeos.

"Smokey gave you everything he had," Mike comments, "and he had a lot of speed and cow. We won several ranch rodeos and ropings, and several of Smokey's fillies are still in the broodmare band today. A lot of my heritage involves running horses with a lot of cow in them."

Mike purchased the Flying A in 1990, and by the time he and Holly married in 2000, both had owned and ridden several Doc O Dynamite horses. They purchased Smart Whiskey Doc, as well as Dynamite Bravo Doc, at John Scott's dispersal sale in Montana. The Majors thought the stallions would cross well on their fast cow horses. "We ride all our fillies to make sure they have trainable minds," Mike explains. "We show some of them, and some go into the broodmare band."

In 2002 Mike began showing in working cow horse events, and then the American

he returned to the headquarters, again legging-up the mule.

Mike's father, who has a real knack for training roping and ranch horses, is principal among Mike's mentors, as was horseman Bob Lee, who introduced Mike to the subtleties of advanced horsemanship and cutting.

"The pastures were 36 sections," Mike explains, "so Bob, the cowboys and I would hit a trot early in the morning and then wait for daylight to gather the cattle. I admired

Quarter Horse Association versatility ranch-horse program came along. "In a sense, I'd been working toward the cow-horse and versatility events all my life," Mike adds.

Playgun- and Docs Stylish Oak-bred horses have since joined the Majors' ranks, as did Love a Little Devil, an own son of Smart Little Lena and out of a Colonel Freckles mare. All wear the Majors' unique "stik-horse" brand, which, Holly explains, "We want to represent the quality and care that go into the horses we raise and train."

Black Hope Stik, a young mare by Smart Whiskey Doc, is a prime representative of the Majors' horse program, worthy of the brand and the name she carries. At the inaugural event, Mike and "Hope" claimed the 2010 Battle in the Saddle Ranch Remuda Champion title and have since earned the inaugural Project Cowboy championship title.

Satisfying and Fun

Make no mistake, the couple's yearling cattle operation on the Flying A and their cow-calf operation in Belen, N. M., are the backbone of Major Cattle Company. But Mike and Holly are pleased that their cow-savvy ranch horses are equally adept in the competitive arena. Mike has enjoyed seeing daily ranch work develop into a sport, and the satisfaction of introducing people to versatile ranch horses has become a real bonus for the longtime cattleman and horseman.

"For the cattlemen and cowboys raised on ranches, all this is an everyday deal. Reading a cow, getting her through a gate or knowing how to hold her is common knowledge in the ranch world," Mike explains. "Good cowboys out there know all those things, but haven't been exposed to the publicity or other things I've been fortunate enough to experience.

"As for the clinics, so often a little thing can help a person and his horse. When things get right, everything feels so good and light, and then the person realizes his horse is really moving and working so much better for him now.

"My philosophy: Show the horse what I want him to do without it being a nightmare for him, so he enjoys doing it. This is simple enough that anybody can do that and get a lot done with horses."

Mike practices what he preaches each time he steps on a horse, no matter if it's a ranch colt or a show-ring veteran. The pay-off is worth his effort.

"Riding these colts we've been raising makes me so appreciative," he continues. "They're a joy to ride. We're trying to bring these cowboy kind of horses back to the show pen. People like the versatility competition, and they like riding pretty horses. So we try to raise horses structurally correct, but good-looking enough to halter, and the horses can perform, too. That's fun."

As for this book, Mike says, "I don't see this as something for a total novice. But I do see this book being for anyone who wants to compete in ranch versatility or to have a really broke and versatile horse, or ranch horse."

Fran Devereux Smith

Working conditions for the versatile ranch horse have changed to include the show arena, and his employer now might be a mainstream recreational rider.

1

FROM RANCH WORK TO RANCH-HORSE COMPETITION

The versatile ranch horse has long been the ideal working partner for those of us in the ranching industry. A half-century or more ago, when the breed associations were being organized, that versatility was admired and respected. It seems we've come full circle all these years later with the popular ranch-versatility competitions. The American Quarter Horse Association, for example, and the American Paint Horse Association now offer ranch-horse events, as do the Ranch Horse Association of America, National Versatility Ranch Horse Association, American Stock Horse Association and other groups.

These versatility events might be popular because horses have become so specialized through the years. Many no longer are the all-around horses like those used back in the 1950s and '60s, when a person could show one in a cow-horse class, roping and halter, too. With the ranch-versatility event, AQHA, for example, can focus on a horse that shows the real disposition and ability of the Quarter Horse, to me, the best horse in the world.

Smart Whiskey Doc's experiences as a working ranch horse contribute greatly to his success as a multiple world champion in ranch-versatility competition.

Not only ranch cowboys, but everybody, from trail riders and trail-class competitors to team ropers, seems to like that old-style versatile horse. Versatility events are set up for a horse that can do a little of everything, plus look good while he does it. He walks, trots and lopes consistently, negotiates trail obstacles, maneuvers like a reining horse, and works a cow and a rope. His balanced conformation makes it easy for him to do these things.

He's a nice-minded, broke horse that anybody, not only a working cowboy, likes to ride. But there also is a lot of appeal in that cowboy part. Most everybody who likes to be horseback has dreamed of sorting and roping cattle, and ranch-versatility competition gives anyone the opportunity to do that.

From Job to Sport

It's been fun to see what ranchers and cowboys have done so long for a living become a sport. For ranch people, maneuvering around an obstacle or having a rope-broke horse is an everyday thing. Ranch

people horseback read a cow and easily send her where they want her to go. They know how she thinks and understand how to use pressure to move or hold her.

That's timing. A top cutting-horse guy is the best because his timing is so perfect. The other part of the equation is that the cutter also feels exactly what his horse is doing and knows when to bring his horse across from one side to the other.

Feel and timing are everything in making a correction, knowing exactly when to put on pressure or take it off a horse or cow. That feel and timing are why a ranch cowboy finds cow work easy in competition; he's spent years developing both. Good cowboys understand timing and feel, and even those riding horses that aren't that great still get the work done because the cowboy's timing is good and he feels when a horse is in the correct position to maneuver easily.

Before versatility events, I competed in the ranch rodeos, and these first began back in the late 1800s. Ranch rodeo events have

"Whiskey," as the stallion Smart Whiskey Doc is known, has set the standard for Major Cattle Company horses when it comes to ranch work and arena competition.

us cowboys realized at first. For example, a cowboy changing leads moved his horse's front end to follow a cow and figured the horse's back end would follow. Most ranch cowboys had good stops on horses, but not the arena slides—just cowboy stops in case we needed to turn the other way to get the job done.

We were amazed at how precise our horses must be when bringing maneuvers from the ranch to the show pen. But that move really has changed cowboy horsemanship for the better, and competitive events give ranch cowboys another reason to work at perfecting their horses.

This shot was taken at the American Quarter Horse Association Versatility Ranch Horse World Championships held during the National Western Stock Show in Denver.

never gone away through the years and, since the Working Ranch Cowboys Association formed, have grown even more popular. At one point, some guys who helped me on the ranch made a good ranch rodeo team, and we did quite well.

WRCA recognizes top ranch horses, as well as top hands, and by 1998 the Ranch Horse Association of America had organized to display a using horse's various talents. Now not only the outfits' colt-starters and trainers compete; all ranch cowboys do. This has led to better horsemanship overall on the ranches, the same as happened when guys like Ray Hunt helped people, ranch cowboys included, understand the horse and get into his mind.

When versatility competition came along, there was a bit more to that than a lot of

Developing basic body-control skills lays the foundation for successful cattle work both on the ranch and in versatility competition.

A New Learning Curve

When most cowboys or horse people with some cattle experience saw their first ranch-versatility event, they figured they could do that. Versatility seemed like working at home, but not exactly.

Before the versatility, I had shown cutting and roping horses. A cutting horse doesn't need to know how to change a lead, and a heading horse needs only his left lead because he's supposed to go left.

Lead changes were a challenge for me, but I didn't really know the correct way to ask a horse for one. Somebody told me to move the horse's hip with my leg, and when I did, my horse darned near swapped ends. He still dropped his shoulder, but I didn't know that. Then I got control of my horse's shoulder and learned I could push his hip and get results in a lead change.

Like her sire, "Whiskey," Black Hope Stik learned the basics while being used for ranch work and has since become successful in the show arena.

Black Hope Stik, aka "Hope," claimed the inaugural 2010 Battle in the Saddle Ranch Remuda Champion title.

*As do many
Major Cattle
Company
horses, the black
mare progressed
from pasture
work to training
for the show
arena.*

The roping skills Hope first learned as a ranch horse became obvious during the 2010 Battle in the Saddle competition.

Lead changes on demand had been foreign to me, and competition made a difference in other ways. My horses could stop and come around, but a correct, flat spin took some work. I had to refine my horse in some respects for the show pen. Timing on maneuvers was part of it, and so were downward transitions. To have a horse really move out and then melt through my hands down to a slow lope—what a great feeling! When I could do that, I knew I was on the road to a well-broke horse.

Even though I could read and handle cattle, being judged was tough at first. On the other hand, show people seem to have a comfort zone in the arena that a ranch cowboy might not have, but the showmen seem leery of cattle. All these things help level the playing field in versatility ranch-horse competition.

A Clinician's Perspective

After I had shown quite a bit in the ranch versatility, initially as an amateur and later

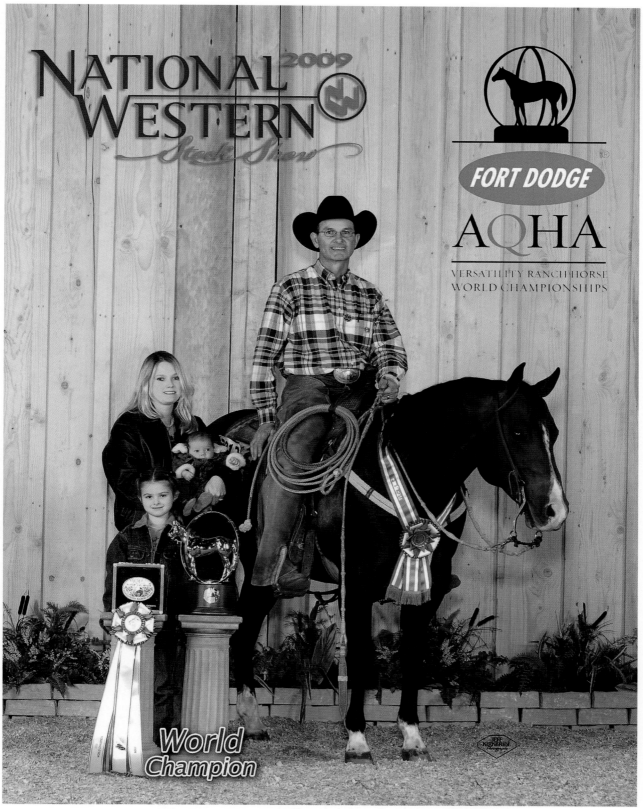

Smart Whiskey Doc has three American Quarter Horse Association world championship titles to his credit—2006 Bayer Select Working Cow Horse World Champion and 2009 and 2010 Versatility Ranch Horse Open World Champion.

Timing And Feel

This bears repeating: Timing and feel are everything, the most important things when it comes to cueing and correcting your horse, or working him on cattle.

Developing good timing and a sensitive feel when you ride is like developing a sixth sense. You learn exactly how much pressure to put on your horse or a cow and learn when to release that pressure. The better your feel and timing, the better you communicate with your horse because he can easily figure out what you want. Your horse has no doubt when he responds correctly because you immediately release the pressure of your cue. Because your horse finds that release, he's willing to respond the next time you cue him, and that creates a good working relationship and pleasant situation for you both.

in the open, my first clinic was in Denver at a March 2007 horse expo on the National Western grounds.

Since then, I've learned the average clinic draws a mix of people. Some ride well, but underestimate themselves; all they need is to refine their horsemanship and build their confidence. Some don't ride well at all, but think they do. Pride keeps them from admitting that they need help. Pride and riding is the worst combination in the world. When a rider throws a leg over a horse, the rider must throw all his pride out the window if he really wants to be a student of the horse.

Most clinic people don't consider how smart horses really are. They're intelligent animals; they don't speak English, but they do have a language. Until we learn their language, we don't ride effectively, and we take our horses for granted.

Horses at clinics are a mix of mares and geldings. Some are overfed, some are under-conditioned, and all need more riding. A horse must be in good bloom and conditioned for versatility competition.

Clinic horses usually are gentle, but few are what I call really responsive, broke horses. A typical horse might be rideable, but that doesn't mean he knows how to move off his rider's leg. Or the horse has been ridden with such heavy hands that he's hard-mouthed; his mouth gaps and his face goes in

the air when the reins are pulled. The horse usually is pretty, but not at all in the bridle. He might pack a bit, but isn't really respectful of it, and few clinic horses can move any given part of their bodies consistently, either forward or back.

At clinics I first show people how to get a horse off the bridle and teach him how to respond, not pull against the reins. When a rider learns how to collect his horse, the rider usually moves to the next level of horsemanship. Timing and feel always come into learning these things, and people at clinics usually gripe about working first on basic control. But by the time we work cattle, everyone realizes how responsive his or her horse can be.

That said, if you can saddle your horse and ride in a lope, the best thing you can do is go to a clinic. With a decent clinician, you should go home with a lot of information. People worry about riding well enough to go to a clinic, but if they never take that step, their horsemanship seldom improves.

A Cattleman's Perspective

At my first clinic I was so unaware of how little knowledge people have about cattle—where to be in position on a cow or what being in that position does to the cow. I've punched cows all my life, and I think I can read cattle as well as anybody, but I had no idea that's what people at clinics really want to learn.

In the versatility class, people are really hurting when it comes to reading cattle. Unfortunately, many people lack the basic maneuverability with their horses that's necessary for working a cow. It's so important to understand that the more responsive a horse is to his rider before starting to work on cattle, the easier and quicker it is for them to partner up and do the cattle work.

That's why this book considers basic horse handling before the cattle work. The better you can maneuver your horse's body, the more successfully you can position your horse on a cow and the more you can expect your horse to rate, stop and turn when the cow makes a move. Working with your horse to improve his responses in the dry work, as it's called, provides the time and interaction necessary to give you both a solid foundation for communicating during the cow work and whenever you ride.

Clear communication between a horse and rider in the "dry" work leads to an effective partnership when working cattle.

No silver-laden saddle or hoof polish required for versatility ranch-horse competition.

2
RANCH-TO-ARENA
FITNESS, GROOMING
AND GEAR

Versatility competition is the exception in a show, as far as gear and grooming are concerned. You don't have to shave every hair from your horse's ears, but if he isn't in top condition, he never catches a judge's eye. Your horse must be fit to complete his versatility work, and his overall body condition is considered in the ranch-horse conformation class.

Workmanlike gear is totally acceptable in versatility events, and a lot of silver isn't necessary. The judges ought to commend any contestant whose saddle shows use, but a filthy saddle is another thing. Demonstrate enough respect for the event to clean your equipment and show the judge your horse and what he can do to the best of your ability.

The comments below about grooming and gear are just that—my comments. These things work for me at a show or on the ranch, but sure aren't the only things that can work in a horse program.

What counts is what works for you.

The Performance Goal

You might not think of fitness, grooming or equipment as part of your performance goal. But to show your horse well in versatility class, he must be in condition; the class asks a lot of a horse. The better he feels physically, the better he responds mentally. Grooming and gear affect the judge's overall impression of you and your horse. Don't

Working gear is totally acceptable in versatility ranch-horse competition.

A horse's overall body condition counts not only in the ranch-horse conformation class, but also determines how well he holds up to the work of versatility competition.

miss that opportunity to show your horse at his best.

Peak Condition

In the versatility world, the conformation class has the same number of points possible as any part, for example, the reining or cutting. The halter competition usually comes at the end of the class, and it's tough to ride a horse all day and keep him looking nice.

You must condition your horse so he still looks great for the conformation class at the end of the day. The judge wants to see any horse in peak condition, too. Overall body condition reflects how fit your horse is, and a horse in great condition physically can do his job, whatever that might be.

- To develop fitness, ride your horse into condition. You must ride him anyway so he listens well through the entire competition. The more you ride, the better your horse's condition and his performance. Once he's fit, maintaining him in top condition isn't hard. The most important thing: Ride your horse.

- When you condition your horse, don't overschool him. It's hard for people to just ride; they can't help doing spins and stops. Then the fitness ride turns into a real training session when the horse needs only a relaxing, conditioning ride.

- Overworking your horse can make him muscle sore and even a little annoyed. In either case, he doesn't perform well at a show. Actually a fresh horse usually shows better than one that has been overschooled.

- Condition your horse by long-trotting and loping him outside the pen, especially the week before a show, to keep his mind fresh. You must keep him listening to you, so work on transitions or suppling exercises, but not a lot of advanced maneuvers.

- Step back and really see your horse. Recognize when he needs more weight, or less, or if he needs muscle tone. You can't change his body type, but when he's in condition, his conformation seems better than it is. So take an objective look and try to show your horse at his best.

Feed's Role

Feed obviously plays a role in a horse's conditioning program. Here at the ranch, we feed straight rolled oats and give our horses a fat supplement. Oats might seem old-fashioned, but there's nothing better to me, and the fat is low-energy.

Feed also makes such a difference in a horse's mental attitude. Nowadays a performance horse often is kept up and fed, but seldom used as he should be. His energy level gets so high and affects his mind to the point that the horse overreacts and overresponds to his rider. That's why my feed program is so important to my training program.

- It's possible to feed and condition a horse without having a "hot" horse. Oats are fairly safe in that respect, and a fat supplement gives a nice bloom to any horse's hair coat and can add a little weight without all the energy.

A fat supplement can help maintain a horse's appearance without creating too much energy, which can get in the way of your training program.

- Avoid hot feeds, anything high-protein, such as corn with protein at 18 percent. Alfalfa puts a bloom on a horse, but, again, a simple fat supplement does that without the energy. About 12 to 14 percent protein is all many horses need, but I do manage my grass hay and alfalfa according to the horse's workload.

- You can't fatten your horse and expect him to manage five versatility classes in one day without riding him into condition.

- The good news: When you ride a too-fat horse into condition, he keeps his bloom and tones his muscles, so he looks really nice for the conformation class.

- It can be hard to keep weight on a horse fit enough to work cattle. It's also hard to ride a thin horse into shape and put weight on him without feeding a lot of energy.

- A horse usually does well with a similar ration each day, but it's not always bad to change his ration. When I can't ride a horse much, I cut back the oats and alfalfa hay, and feed more grass hay to keep his energy level manageable. Otherwise, it takes a half-day to get his mind really responsive. I want my horse in solid physical shape, but I want his mind in good shape, too.

Elementary Coat Care

When a horse is in condition, his hair coat has a bloom, but the elements can tarnish that shiny coat. It's natural for a horse to sweat salt in the summer and to grow a heavy winter coat, and both affect how great your horse looks.

- When it's hot, rinse your horse with water after you ride. Left in his coat, salt and sweat really dull his hair. How often you bathe your horse before a show is up to you, but if it's really dusty in your area, you might put a sheet on your horse when you haul him.

- Using blankets and neck sweats to keep horsehair slick is a lot of work. If you do that, the old-style blanket with only the two back straps is easy and fast to put on and take off a horse. That style blanket might slide a little, but not enough to be a real problem.

- Using lights in the barn is another way to help keep your horse from developing a winter hair coat. Be careful; your horse can get the seasons mixed up and grow long hair in the summertime. For a slick coat during winter shows, you might let him grow a little hair in August and September, and then change the schedule with lights in October.

- To successfully manage winter hair growth, be aware of how many hours of artificial light your horse gets. Put your lights on timers and use a light meter to check how much light is in your barn. A fluorescent light must be 100 lumens to make a horse think it's daylight and fool his system. Two 100-watt bulbs in a stall can help minimize hair growth, and so do two 150-watt fluorescent bulbs in long fixtures.

Rinse off your horse to keep sweat and salt from dulling his hair.

Ears, Manes, Muzzles and More

The nice thing about ranch versatility: Grooming, like the equipment used in this class, can be more using horse than show horse. Clipping and trimming a ranch horse for show isn't as fussy a deal as closely shaving a horse for a regular halter class.

- A trim, not a shave, is sufficient when grooming your horse's ears and muzzle for a versatility ranch-horse class. In fact, AQHA rules discourage trimming inside the ears, but at least clip the long ear and muzzle hair. How closely you clip your horse is your call.

- A bridle path is optional for versatility horses. Not having a bridle path might seem natural, more like a cow horse, but that depends on the horse. If a bridle path complements your horse and makes his neck and throatlatch look slim, you might want to clip him. (See "Preview the Look" before you start cutting.)

- The smoother your horse's mane, the nicer he looks. A flat, smooth mane helps a neck that's a little thick look better than it really is.

- Use conditioner to help manage mane hair, but if that doesn't do the job, try braiding or banding your horse's mane, or use a "snuggy" around your horse's neck to smooth his mane. Remember to pull take out the bands and braids before you show; they aren't legal in the show arena.

Preview the Look

A bridle path is optional in versatility classes, but if you clip one and don't like it, waiting for your horse's mane to grow seems to take forever. If you think your horse might look good with a bridle path or that a longer one might complement his neck, preview the look before you start clipping.

- First, estimate the length of the bridle path you might cut. An old rule of thumb suggests the length of the horse's ear.

- Starting behind your horse's ears, comb the amount of mane you might trim to the opposite side and then rubber-band or braid it. Now stand on the side where the mane naturally hangs to determine if the bridle path change improves your horse's looks.

- If you like what you see, you know how much mane to clip. If you think a longer bridle path might be better, simply band or braid a little more mane for another preview. If you don't like what you see, pull out the rubber bands or braids.

Determine what length bridle path best complements your horse's neck by braiding his mane to the offside before you pick up your clippers.

Trimming a bridle path is optional for ranch-versatility competition.

- Mane and tail care takes as much time as you want to spend. If your horse's mane and tail are really coarse and dry, try a conditioner to help revive and soften the hair. Mane and tail conditioners have come a long way from the WD-40 used years ago to untangle hair.

- If your horse switches out a lot of tail hair, loose-braid his tail or tie it in a knot at home, so he doesn't lose as much hair. Plus, he's less apt to step on his tail and pull out more hair.

- If you don't like the waves a braid puts in your horse's tail, undo the braid before the class and spray his tail with water to relax the waves.

Leg and Hoof Care

When grooming a versatile ranch horse's legs and hoofs, again, the approach is more using-horse than show-horse—no hoof polish allowed. When it comes to trimming leg hair, do what suits you, and understand that nothing is as critical in the versatility as your horse's overall condition and soundness, not even how closely his legs are trimmed.

- Some people trim fetlocks closely, and others trim the front legs, but only long hairs on the hind legs. The thinking: The hair is there for protection when a horse stops, although skid boots can be used in the versatility reining or cutting.

- Although hoof polish isn't allowed in ranch-versatility events, never ignore your horse's hoof care. Keep his feet in good shape, clean and healthy, no matter if your horse is trimmed or shod.

- When shoeing your horse, try to weigh every aspect of the class, not what someone else does. Selecting shoes for a versatility horse is tough. He can score higher in the reining if he slides, but slide plates really hinder a horse in cutting. He can't take hold of the ground to turn, and if he loses the cow, there are deductions in your score.

- Slide plates for the versatility reining class aren't critical now, and that's the only time plates can help in the five classes. In a reined or working cow-horse event, everyone needs a long slide to score well. That's not the deal yet in

Trying This and That

I've tried everything to make a horse's shoes work for both versatility reining and cutting. I've drilled holes in shoes and tapped in bolts to give some grip when the horse needs it, then have taken out the bolts when he doesn't. I've welded beads across the toe of a shoe and along the sides for grip, and then ground off the beads after the cutting so my horse could slide in the reining.

I've replaced regular nails with ice nails for grip. I've added extra nail holes at the back of shoes for spikes to help get traction in the cutting pen, and also tried screw-in deals. But those threads must be plugged to stay clean, so the screw can be reused.

Now I usually use ⅞-inch sliding plates on the back feet, but I've even ridden horses with regular keg shoes at the Quarter Horse world show.

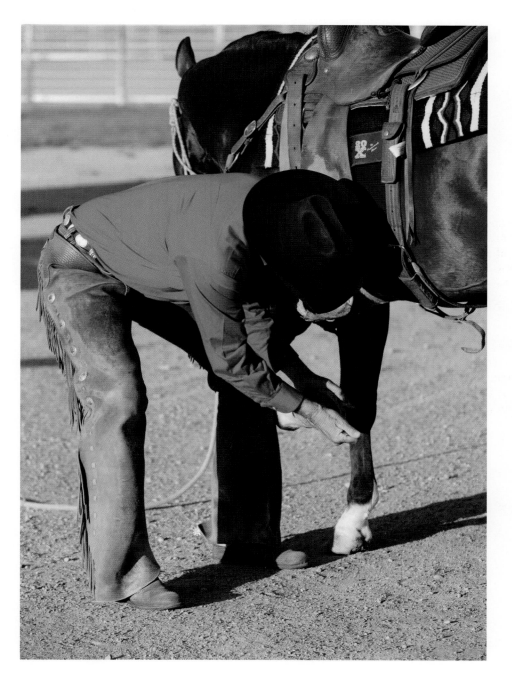

Routine hoof care is necessary to maintain any horse in top condition.

"Keep his feet in good shape, clean and healthy, no matter if your horse is trimmed or shod."

ranch versatility, but down the road probably could be. What is important is that your horse stops in frame and drops his butt, and that might be only a short slide, depending on the ground.

- Everyone wants his horse to stop and slide, but the ground in most arenas seldom allows those long slides. When the ground isn't good, don't ask your horse to stop hard. If it hurts him, he soon quits trying to stop.

- For the average person showing in ranch versatility, a wide keg shoe usually works fine, and a ⅞-inch sliding plate, if necessary, isn't bad.

Halters

"Workmanlike" describes the equipment used for showing in the versatility ranch-horse class. A horse shown in the versatility conformation class should look like he's in condition to do the work of a ranch horse, and the gear on him should look like it can hold up to the work.

- Versatility rules first called for a rope halter to be used in the conformation class. Now a flat nylon halter, plain leather one or rope halter is acceptable although silver trim is discouraged.

- A rope halter gives a little more control than a flat nylon or leather halter, and

A braided rawhide noseband on a halter focuses pressure to give more control than a plain rope or flat nylon noseband provides.

The Ring Halter

Most rope halters have a knot under the horse's chin, where the lead rope fastens, but the rope halters I make have a ring that slides under a horse's chin. When I longe a horse and his head is out of position, the ring really helps bring his face toward me.

With a regular rope halter, the fiador knot under a horse's chin pulls on his face, but his nose can tilt to the outside of the circle. With the ring, as I pull on the line, the ring slides, the knots on the side of the halter put pressure on my horse's nose, and he gives his entire face to find a release from pressure.

Plus, if I need to put a horse on a hot walker, I can use a snap in the halter ring. Some people don't like snaps, but they are convenient.

The halter ring helps keep a horse's nose in the desired position when being longed.

a rope halter with a braided rawhide noseband can give even more control with more focused pressure.

- Some rope halters have brass tips on the end of the rope you tie over your horse's poll. Brass is hard and the tail of the rope could hit your horse's eye. Tuck that tail end underneath the halter throatlatch piece to keep the tail from flopping against your horse's face, and always be sure you know how to fasten a rope halter correctly.

- You also can stretch a piece of clear pipe or poly hose with needle-nosed pliers just enough to pull the brass ends on a rope halter through the pipe or hose. That little piece also helps to keep the ends even.

Pads and Blankets

Some blankets nowadays feel just a little lightweight to me. When I was a kid, we drove 40 miles through the Navajo reservation to our ranch. They sheared the sheep and made the blankets, and nothing is better on a horse's back.

- When your saddle sits correctly on your horse's back, almost any blanket or pad works fine. If the saddle doesn't fit like it should, no blanket, no matter how expensive, does much good.

- Not many blankets or pads seem to work that great until they've had a little use and wear. After you break in a blanket, the padding takes shape so it fits your horse. That shape helps keep your saddle still and quiet on your horse's back.

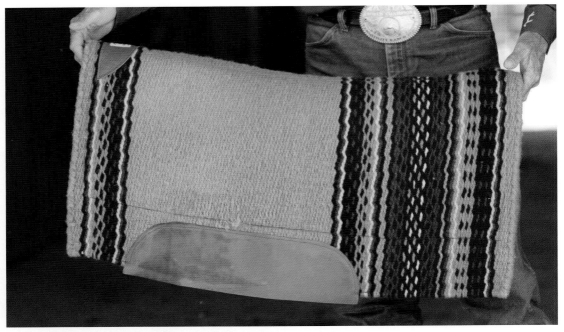

Most blankets and pads require a bit of use before they take shape and really fit a horse's back.

- Old-time Navajo blankets still set the standard. Nothing is better than a wool Navajo on a horse's back. The natural wool absorbs sweat, but it's heavy when it's wet and can take a long time to dry.

- A popular combination pad is a felt one with a fleece bottom and a Navajo rug on top. There's enough cushion with the felt and fleece to take some shock when you rope, and the pad sits on your horse without rolling around on his back. That's important, no matter how pretty the pad.

- Another combination pad uses only the fleece with a Navajo top, with no felt between the two. Without the felt, the pad is softer, but it does seem to roll a little on a horse's back, which makes your saddle roll, too.

- Blankets designed primarily for cutting horses usually are really soft and supple to give close contact with a horse. However, other blanket and pad styles put more padding between your horse and the saddle.

- A contoured pad that easily shapes to fit a horse's back has a Navajo or canvas top and wool felt bottom, with a split in the middle that leaves an air pocket up and down your horse's spine. This type blanket has padding where it needs to be and really fits the shape of a horse's back from the start. Breaking in most blankets and pads usually takes 15 or 20 rides.

Saddles

There is no right or wrong saddle to ride in a versatility ranch-horse class. The main things are that you can keep your seat in your saddle and that it is comfortable for you and your horse.

Versatility ranch-horse rules actually call for workmanlike equipment. Think about any new cowboy coming to a ranch. If he has a brand-new saddle, bridle and chaps, you can bet he's just starting and not a good cowboy yet. But when a cowboy shows up with working equipment that has seen use, you can bet he knows his job.

Your well-used equipment shows a judge that you ride your horse. To become really good in any event, you must use your gear, and that means riding your horse.

- A saddle should sit deep on a horse's back, not rest high on his withers, and have contact from the withers through the end of the tree. No saddle can completely conform to a horse's back. A horse couldn't turn a steer or do a rollback if the saddle totally kept him from bending through his middle.

- So many people dally rope today that most saddles don't have to take much jerk. But when a cowboy ropes a 1,200-pound bull, throws him 20 feet of rope and goes the other way with his rope tied on the horn, it takes a strong-built saddle to take the jerk and hold the bull when he hits the end of the rope.

- A roping saddle isn't ideal for ranch versatility because many are built low in the front end, which throws you forward. The horn rides down low on your horse, so the rope pressure doesn't pull so directly on the withers. However, a roping saddle's low cantle doesn't help you keep your seat that well.

- Cutout saddles minimize the leather underneath your legs to give you close contact with your horse. That's fine for riding a mature horse. If you ride a young horse, you might not like a cutout as well, maybe because the colt hasn't filled out yet.

- A ranch-cutter saddle gives good contact with a horse. The big difference between a ranch cutter and a regular cutting saddle is the horn. The cutting saddle horn is taller, and the way the horn ties into the saddle and the rigging aren't made to take much jerk.

- The ranch-cutter horn isn't as tall as a cutter's horn or the dally horn in a roping saddle, but the makers have beefed up the ranch-cutter tree and rigging. When you train horses, a very tall horn can get in the way, especially when you ride two-handed.

- If you work cattle all day, there's no comparison between sitting in a ranch cutter and a traditional roping saddle. The ranch cutter is the more comfortable ride when you're horseback a long time.

- All ranch cutters aren't the same. A favorite of mine has a 3½-inch cantle and a deep seat with a Buster Welch front end, which allows really good contact with a horse. There's enough

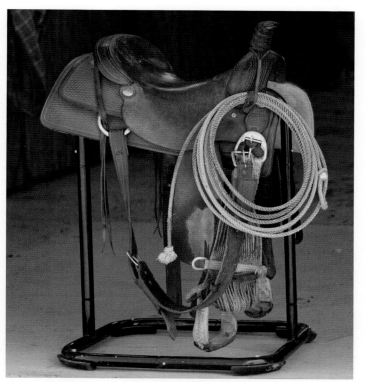

This is a Sean Ryon saddle that I use for working on the ranch and when I'm showing in versatility classes.

I also ride this Vinton saddle a lot. Like the Sean Ryon saddle, this saddle also has a wrapped post horn.

saddle to hold me in there when I go down the fence to turn a cow. Another ranch cutter I have is built up in front, and a third style is flatter in front, but could be shaped differently where my legs hang. It's all a matter of personal preference.

Breast Collars

I don't necessarily use a breast collar all the time, but I do on a round-backed horse or one with big shoulders that tend to push a saddle back. As a horse gets older and has more power on cattle, I use a breast collar, but I seldom use one on a colt.

- Breast-collar fit is the thing. Nothing should rub your horse, no matter the breast-collar style you like.

- The breast collar should fit above the points of your horse's shoulders. If it's too loose, the breast collar can slip down over the points and rub your horse's shoulders. The attachments for some decorations or trim can eat into your horse's shoulders, too.

- Your breast collar shouldn't be so tight that it chokes your horse. The "V" should rest at the base of your horse's throat, not on it.

The Flat-Braided Breast Collar

I'm particular about my breast collars, and the only breast collar I use now isn't even a traditional leather one. It's made of a double row of flat-braided rope that's sewn together and simply doesn't rub a horse. I bought two of those breast collars at the farm and ranch store about 20 years ago, and, unfortunately, they're the only ones I've ever seen made like that. This particular breast collar stays down and in place, so it doesn't choke my horse. The flat braid doesn't rub him, and there's no big buckle in the middle to rub.

- The tie-down strap between your horse's legs helps keep the V out of his throat, but the strap shouldn't be so tight that it rubs between your horse's legs.

- Some saddles have D-rings fastened high on the skirts, and attaching the breast-collar tugs, or straps, there helps keep it positioned correctly. However, sometimes the rings are too high for a good fit.

- Some breast collars attach to the dees in your saddle rigging, but those can be too low for a good fit.

- With a breast collar that has two tugs on each side, fasten one to the D-ring in the skirt and the other to the rigging dee. That gives plenty of room for adjustment.

- If your breast collar has only one tug on each side, and you need more adjustment, add a second set of tugs so you can place your breast collar where it needs to be.

Leg Gear

Splint, bell and skid boots all have a place in my horse program, but using protective leg gear on a horse sometimes is like using a neck sweat or winter blanket—way too many straps. The leg wraps I like best are those that are easy to put on a horse.

- Splint boots protect. The easy-to-fasten type of boots usually have some type of foam padding to protect your horse's cannon bone and only two straps that fasten with hook-and-loop closures. This boot protects your horse if one front leg bumps the other when your horse turns or works a cow. If you ride a lot of horses every day, but don't stress any one horse a long time, these quick-to-use splint boots might be the thing.

- Splint boots support, but some seem hard to use because several straps have to be fastened in certain ways. This type boot does more than protect your horse's cannon bone by supporting the entire structure. Use this type of splint boot when you ask a lot of your horse and he's working for a long time.

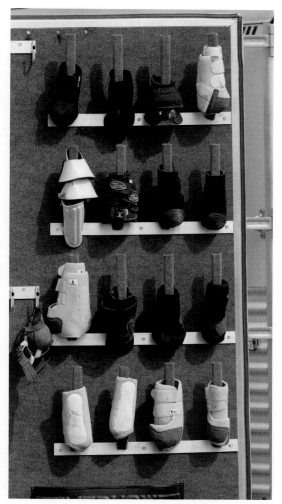

Gear that can protect and support your horse's legs is some of the least expensive insurance you can buy to help keep your riding program on track.

- Bell boots are relatively cheap insurance that can keep you in business. If your horse overreaches with a hind leg and strikes the bulb on the back of his front foot, you're out of the competition. It pays to use bell boots when you can at a show although no one is allowed to use them in the trail or western riding parts of versatility competition. Anytime your horse must go in fast, forward motion or work a cow, it's a good idea to put bell boots on your horse, even when working in your arena at home.

- Skid boots prevent your horse from burning his hind legs, no matter if the ground is really hard or great for

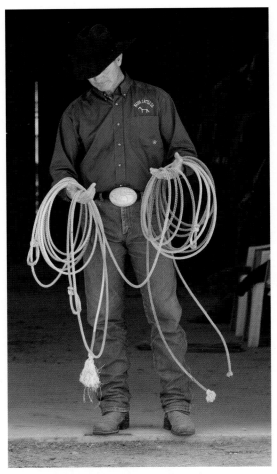

The type rope you purchase affects how comfortably and easily you learn to handle a rope for versatility competition.

about how you do that. (See the later chapter, "Learn the Ropes.")

- The type rope you purchase affects how comfortably you learn to handle a rope well. Try a poly rope, not a nylon. The weight of a poly rope seems to work and feel better for novice ropers, more broken-in from the start, so it makes practicing easier than a nylon does.

- A poly rope in the standard 28-foot length works fine for most people in ranch versatility. The poly is easy to handle and better suited for muleys, the cattle without horns that are used most in the versatility cow work.

- A poly rope has a little more dip in the loop, when it's delivered, which makes it easier to catch a 600- or 700-pound muley because you throw the loop down and over a muley's head instead of bringing it across a steer's horns like a team roper would.

- When a nylon rope hits a muley, the loop often bounces, which can cause a miss, and the nylon loop really doesn't stay as flat as it should for a smooth catch.

- Many people never rope enough to feel comfortable using a nylon. Their arms get sore, and before long, they quit trying to rope or don't rope unless they're competing.

- A little practice at home goes a long way toward building muscles and muscle memory.

stopping. Arena ground is seldom such that a versatility horse can make long, sliding stops, but it never hurts to protect your horse's fetlocks with skid boots.

- Keep your leg gear clean so dried mud and burrs don't irritate your horse's legs.

- Leg gear can't help your horse if you don't use it. Take care of your horse's legs.

Ropes

It takes time to build the strength to use a rope and to build the muscle memory to become a consistent roper in the working ranch-horse class. The best way to do that is by handling your rope a little every day until using it becomes almost a subconscious thing, like driving a car. Then you feel your rope and make a correction without really thinking

Ropes are available to suit people of all ages and at all levels of expertise.

Any bit or training tool becomes what you make of it.

3

BITS, BITTING AND HEADGEAR

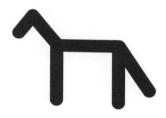

In all reality, a bridle—the bit—is what you make of it. The bridle is a function of your hands. If your hands are too fast or too hard, it makes no difference what bridle and bit you use; it isn't the right one. No bit is any softer or harsher than your hands. Horsemanship comes down to that.

The biggest problems people, especially novice riders, have with horses result when hands are too quick and aggressive on the reins. Instead of picking up softly on the bit and letting the horse feel it before asking him to move, the rider's hands move fast. That comes across as a jerk to the horse. The rider doesn't make contact with his horse or teach him anything, but only jerks the horse into doing something.

The next big problem for any horse packing a bit happens when his mouth is sore. Very little pressure on a bit can cause him pain. Bitting problems also result when training tools, such as cavessons and martingales, are improperly adjusted or when a rider relies on the tool, rather than teaching his horse to pack a bit.

Like everyone, I have many bits on my wall. I've never been so narrow-minded to think that one bit or one way of doing things is absolutely better than another. If my mind's not broad enough to see the good in each and gather the concept, I've quit learning.

But I have learned that I tend to use five bits the most: D-ring, egg-butt or ring snaffle; D-ring twisted-wire snaffle; low-port shanked bit with swivel sides; high-port shanked bit with swivel sides; and a bit with a chain mouthpiece. My comments on these bits and others are below, and my experiences might not be the same as those other people have with their horses and bits.

Meanwhile, I'm still looking for that perfect bit. It must be out there somewhere.

Horsemanship comes down to the rider's hands, not the bit in a horse's mouth.

My Top Five Bits

D-ring, O-ring, or egg-butt snaffle bit
D-ring, twisted-wire snaffle bit
Bit with chain mouthpiece
Low-port shanked bit with swivel sides
High-port shanked bit with swivel sides

The Performance Goal

More than anything, the headgear you use on your horse and how you handle that headgear affect your ranch versatility score. Riding a light, responsive horse is a true display of horsemanship, and a judge recognizes that when he sees it.

If your horse isn't responsive and light, you can help change that. Simply floating his teeth might make a big difference; teaching him to be soft in hand can lead to real change. Instead of stepping up to a heavy bit, go back to a mild one and teach your horse to be light. Afterward, when you advance to a signal-type bit, your horse can understand the signals you give.

Caps, Points and Wolf Teeth

When you have a bitting problem, first check your horse's teeth, especially with a 3-year-old, but even a grown horse can have problems. Float his teeth when necessary. He bridles up better than he did and puts his feed to good use with less waste, so his body condition is easy to maintain.

- A long 2- or 3-year-old horse can have caps on the first three bottom and three top teeth on each side, and caps mess up a bitting program. The difference between riding a colt before he pops off a cap and afterward is unbelievable. He comes to the bridle because his pain is gone and he's willing to perform.

- A bit barely touching a loose cap can hurt, and a cap can have needle-sharp prongs pushing into a colt's gum. When you pull on the bit, those points hurt, especially with a snaffle. A snaffle pulls up and into the corners of a horse's mouth, where a flap of skin inside his lip can be pinched on a point, but a shanked bit has a different pull.

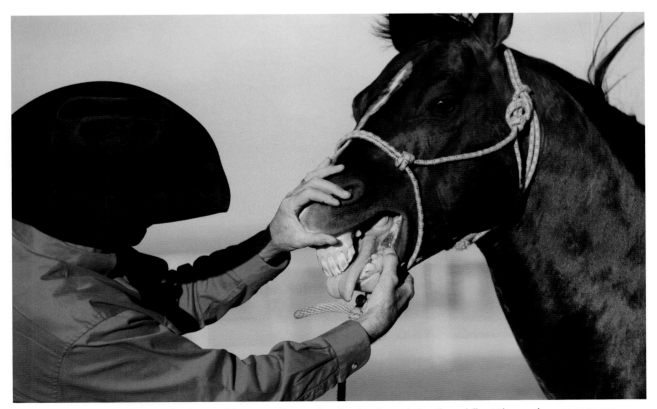

Dental problems often cause bitting problems, so it pays to check a horse's teeth and float them when necessary.

- Check each side of your horse's mouth, top and bottom, for visible caps. Remove any caps you find so your horse can comfortably carry his bit.

- Wolf teeth are right in front of a horse's molars. Having a wolf tooth is like having a loose tooth—any pressure hurts. Even if the bit doesn't contact the tooth, a horse's lip can be pinched between the tooth and bit, and his first response usually is to throw his head.

- People often remove colts' wolf teeth when they're castrated, but some colts are 2 before wolf teeth develop. Although mares usually don't have wolf teeth, some do.

- Run your thumb along your horse's gum from the bar to the first molar, on the top and bottom. Most wolf teeth are above, but occasionally can be on the bottom. If your horse reacts strongly to your touch, a wolf tooth probably needs to be pulled.

- A horse of any age can have points develop from wear on his teeth, and those sharp points cut into his cheeks and gums. Even a well-trained, mature horse fights the bit when his mouth hurts.

- Watch for signs of teeth problems. If your horse often drops feed on the ground, he might not be able to chew easily because of points. When you pick up the reins, if your horse at first seems to respond, then stiffens or fights his head, check the teeth. Something probably is hurting his mouth and affecting his response.

The Simple Snaffle

I start every horse in a D-ring, egg-butt or O-ring snaffle, and I could ride a horse in a snaffle bit until he darned near died of old age. Here are a few things to consider when riding with a snaffle bit.

- The more curved a snaffle mouthpiece, the softer the bit because the shape conforms to the horse's mouth. The straighter the mouthpiece, the less it conforms and the more pressure the horse can feel.

A snaffle bit, no matter if it's a D-ring like the one shown, an O-ring or an egg-butt, is ideal for starting a young horse.

- A mouthpiece made of large stock is less severe than a mouthpiece made of small, thin stock.

- A snaffle bit has virtually the same pull on your horse's mouth that you feel in your hands. The pull lifts the bit up and into the mouth, and that's when a horse usually drops his face and flexes at the poll. The pressure points are in those corners of your horse's mouth, his lips, and when he learns to break at the poll, the pull changes to put some slight pressure on the bars.

- A D-ring snaffle bit also puts slight pressure on the offside of your horse's head when you pull a rein. That offside pressure helps bring his nose around in the direction you want. An egg-butt snaffle does that, too, but that doesn't happen so much with an O-ring snaffle.

- Ride your horse with a snaffle bit until he tells you it's time to change. He might push against your hands or feel heavier in hand, which means your control is gone, so his response is lacking.

The Twisted-Wire Snaffle

Here at the ranch, I ride many horses, and stallions tend to become a little stiff with a smooth snaffle. When a horse gets heavy in hand, I swap to a snaffle bit with a twisted-wire mouthpiece. When I do, I keep the following things in mind.

- A twisted-wire snaffle is only a short-term tool to be used for a few days. When you make the switch, flex your horse quite a bit, doing the exercises described in later chapters, to remind him to be light. After a few days, switch back to the regular snaffle, and your horse should be responsive.

- Like a martingale or cavesson, a twisted-wire snaffle is a good tool for teaching your horse, but one that can't be used in the show arena.

- Don't overuse or abuse a twisted-wire snaffle; yanking on it only makes a horse heavy in hand and dead in the mouth. Instead, work with the bit and your horse to teach him lightness. You can train your horse to be light in hand, the same as you teach him to be heavy by pulling on a bit. How to lighten your horse's response is covered in later chapters.

Make the Transition

People often ask how to tell when it's time to switch a horse from the snaffle bit and bridle him in a shanked bit. The correct answer depends on how well a horse and rider understand a few basic concepts, including slow hands, signal time, leverage and pressure. When I keep those things in mind and do my homework in the snaffle bit, the transition usually is easy.

- When you school your horse and signal him, the concept of slow hands means that your hands move slowly, so your horse has time to figure out what the

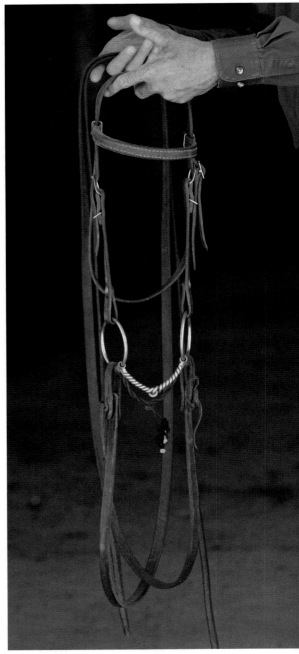

A twisted-wire snaffle can be used for a few days to help lighten a horse that's become heavy in hand.

signal means. Switch to a shanked bit only when your hands are slow and quiet. Then your horse remains quiet.

- With a snaffle, when you take slack out of the reins, there's a lot of hand movement before you make contact with your horse's mouth. That delay, or long signal time, gives him time to figure out a change is coming.

- With slow hands and ample signal time, a horse learns to be light because he's never attacked with the bit. People often attack when a horse seems slow to respond or makes a mistake, and that scares a horse.

- A shanked bit adds leverage, which increases the pressure of your pull in your horse's mouth. A pound of pull from your hand might, for example, be a 5-pound pull on your horse's mouth. The concept of leverage is a good one because ideally you use the leverage to signal lightly and never get forceful with your hands.

- A shanked bit's signal is quicker than the snaffle's signal because of leverage, and a horse learns to respond faster. Even the shape of the shank can affect the signal time. A straight shank has a quicker signal than a curved shank because it takes longer for the curved-shank bit to make contact in a horse's mouth.

- With shanks and a curb strap or chain on a bridle, bit pressure goes to the bars in a horse's mouth and on the curb strap or chain. If the mouthpiece doesn't have much tongue-relief, pressure also is applied to a horse's tongue, but most horses are comfortable without that. An extremely high mouthpiece can put pressure on the horse's palate, but that's a signal bit for a finished horse, not for everyday training. A horse must be trained to respond to pressure before you use a signal bit.

- When your horse understands pressure, he knows what to do when you squeeze him up and into the bridle with your legs, and pick up on the reins. He flexes his poll, so his nose is more on the vertical, and his spine is soft. He learns those things in the snaffle bit.

- When your horse flexes and softens consistently in the snaffle, you can switch to a shanked bit. Although your horse might bump against the different bit a little at first, he easily figures out the response you want and should come right back to your hands with few problems.

- When any horse, even a colt in a snaffle, pushes hard against your hands, you might want to try a shanked bit. Be careful to use your hands very lightly, really show the horse what you want, and make sure he stays off the bit.

The Chain Bit

When I take a colt out of a snaffle bit, a short-shanked bit with a chain mouthpiece, even without the curb strap, can work well for the transition, especially when it's an easy day's ride so the colt can get accustomed to the bit. Because it's an easy ride and the chain is pleasant to the horse, a colt soon begins to understand the different pressure points with this bit, as compared with a snaffle. People have misconceptions about the chain mouthpiece, but most horses seem to like it, even the few that don't seem to like any bridle.

- Use the chain bit with a leather curb strap. You might even take the curb strap completely off the bit and try it in an enclosed area at first. Without the curb, a chain bit is more like a gag bit, with a slower signal than the chain bit has with the curb fastened.

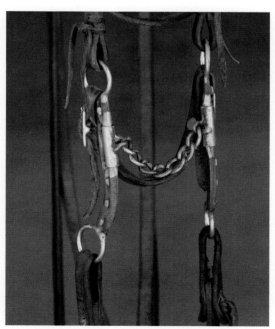

Horses seem content with the chain bit, maybe because it flexes and conforms to any horse's mouth without creating a "hot spot," where the pressure is more intense.

- Ride your horse lightly at first and let him get accustomed to and figure out the chain bit.

- When you make the transition to any bit, the main thing is to let your horse find his relief. Pick up the reins and hold your horse. Don't go to war with him—just wait. He soon learns to find relief when he gives the correct response, and then you release him.

- Horses don't play with the chain links in the mouthpiece, but are content to carry the bit, maybe because there's no particular "hot spot," where the chain applies more pressure to a specific area.

- Because the chain flexes and breaks all the way across the mouthpiece, the bit conforms well to any horse's mouth and is less severe than a ported bit.

- A caution: Be sure the chain lays flat in your horse's mouth. If the chain is positioned incorrectly and attached to a bit at the wrong angle, the edge of the chain could rub your horse's tongue.

- Another caution: Although a nice training bit, a chain bit isn't legal to use in the show arena.

The Low-Port, Short-Shanked Bit

This low-port, solid-mouthpiece, short-shanked bit is s broken on the sides and swivels. Most colts with 90 to 100 saddles probably would ride fairly well in this loose-sided bit, if necessary. This low-port bit is all some 4- and 5-year-old horses ever need although they usually continue to work well in the snaffle bit, as well.

- Because the shanks swivel at the ends of the mouthpiece, the signal to your horse isn't as abrupt as it can be with a stiff bit.

- With loose shanks, it's also easy to pull your horse's face to the side to help lead him into a turn.

- When the shanks are aluminum, the bit is lightweight, so it doesn't seem like a big deal to your horse.

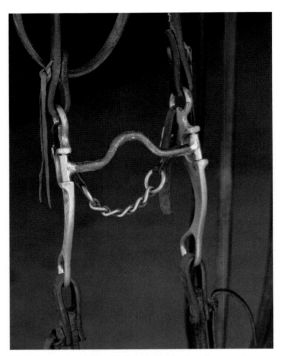

This low-port bit with its swivel shanks creates a slower signal than a stiff bit with no swivel, or play, in the shanks.

- After you ride with the shanked bit awhile, you might want to go back to your snaffle, and then bounce back and forth between the two bits.

The High-Port Shanked Bit

This high-port bit gives a horse plenty of tongue relief, which I like. Plus, the bit fits more horses better than any bridle I've ever used. Older horses get along well with it, and when I pick up the reins while using the bit on a young horse, this bit doesn't scare him, and he responds. For overall, day-in and day-out riding, this bit usually gets more results than anything and probably is the best all-around bridle I have.

- The high-port aluminum bit with swivel sides is very similar to the short-shanked bit mentioned previously, but has more port, about 1½ inches, in the mouthpiece for tongue relief.

- The shank on the high-port bit, slightly longer than the shank on the low-port bit, provides a little more leverage.

The key to using a high-port bit, which gives a horse tongue relief, is properly adjusting the curb strap.

- When you use a high-port bit, adjust your curb strap correctly. The curb should tighten as the port moves up toward the palate. Then the pressure affects the bars, curb and palate, preferably with very light pressure on all three.

Other Bits

Bits can have high, medium or low ports, different types of mouthpieces and long or short shanks, and the mouthpieces can be made from big stock or small. I use the five bits described above the most, but have many types of bits on my barn wall, and each has its place. Every horse is different, just as every rider is different. What suits one horse might not suit the next one I ride, and the bit that works for me in my program might not work for someone else.

Finding a suitable bit for a horse depends so much on a rider's hands and how a horse has been prepared to accept and pack a bit in his mouth. Below are a few other bits on my barn wall. I don't use these bits all the time, but do ride with one when it seems to suit a particular horse.

- A short-shanked gag bit with noseband and broken mouthpiece can suit some horses, especially when making the transition to a shanked bit. I have two gag bits like this, one with a snaffle mouthpiece and another with a chain. This combination bit has rings on the ends of the mouthpiece, and the broken mouthpieces are very forgiving. With only a little pressure, the mouthpiece moves on the rings, like a gag bit, which gives a horse time to figure out things before he really feels the effects. These two bits aren't show-ring legal, but do provide a long, slow signal for the horse, and that makes these bits good for a person with fast hands.

- Many people use a shanked bit with a snaffle mouthpiece. However, when the reins are picked up, the shanks come together, and the mouthpiece makes a V with pressure on a horse's tongue. If that

With slight pressure from the reins, this mouthpiece moves on the rings, like a gag bit. That creates a slow signal that gives a horse time to figure out what his next move should be.

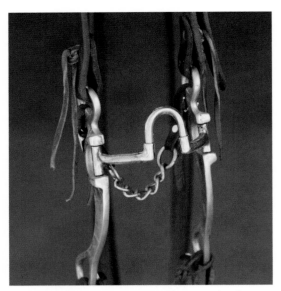

Because a horse tends to gap his mouth when ridden with a correctional bit, caution should be used to keep the horse from developing a gapping habit.

happened to me, I'd throw my head, too, so I seldom use this bit although I try it occasionally. A solid slobber bar on the shanks can help keep that V from being so extreme.

- The correctional bit seems to work best with stallions that tend to get heavy on the bit, but the way the bit pulls a horse's mouth down automatically teaches him to open it, so I don't use this bit much. I

don't want my horse to learn to gap his mouth. This bit is legal for showing.

- The cathedral bit is for a true bridle horse, a mature horse that's been taught about pressure and how to respond to it. In the reined cow horse world, a rider wants to be able to tie his bridle reins to the shanks with a fine string and his horse be totally responsive. That's how subtle a rider can be with a true bridle horse.

- My one correctional cathedral-style bit is legal in the show arena, and I've used it a few times when a horse gets show-smart and ring-savvy. That's not to say the horse is bad; he wants to get the job done, but on his terms—a little faster and a little pushier than usual. A horse backs off this bit, which isn't as severe as it looks if a horse knows how to be soft in the bridle. Even then, with this bit a horse tends to gap his mouth when the reins are pulled.

- In the reined cow-horse part at the World's Greatest Horseman, the rules stated I must have a roller on my bit. I didn't, so I built and welded a roller onto a purchased bit, added a slobber-bar at the bottom and changed the angle of the mouthpiece. When I look through those bridle rings, where the headstall fastens, I should be able to see the mouthpiece, which is about where it should be on a balanced bit.

Know the Rules

My wife, Holly, who also competes in ranch-versatility classes, points out that at shows people often are disqualified simply because they're unfamiliar with rules about bits and curbs that are legal in the competitive arena.

A common cause for disqualification is a twisted curb chain that doesn't lay flat and smooth against the horse's chin. It doesn't matter if the chain has been twisted intentionally for additional control or fastened incorrectly from ignorance; any judge automatically disqualifies the competitor.

Association rulebooks typically specify the ports and shank length for acceptable bits. Within those guidelines, a horse's age also can affect the legal and appropriate headgear. Even the use of romal and split reins in the arena must follow association rules.

Bitting rules can apply to specific classes, as well. In a National Reined Cow Horse Association bridle class, for example, a romal must be used. The bit must have a slobber bar and a roller in the mouthpiece, and a metal rivet on the chinstrap is illegal.

Know the rules when you compete so you don't get disqualified for your equipment.

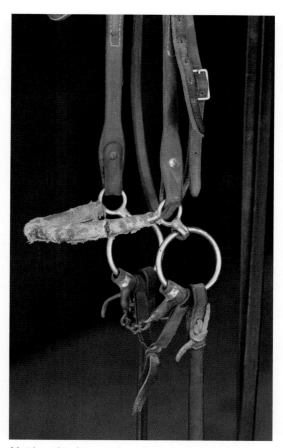

Neither this bit nor the other similar bit shown is legal in the show arena, but either can help a horse understand a rider with fast hands.

- If you don't want your horse to rub off his headgear, use a browband bridle with a throatlatch. If your horse rubs his head on something, the throatlatch can help keep the bridle on him.

- One-eared headstalls are fine for show or at home and come with or without throatlatches. This type headstall works best when you ride one-handed on a more finished horse. I never use a one-eared headstall with a snaffle bit.

- A split-ear headstall is a one-eared headstall, just a different design. The split should be wide enough and long enough to comfortably fit around your horse's ear without rubbing or irritating your horse anywhere.

- The spade bit is used only as a signal bit on a finished horse. In the California tradition, a two-rein horse is ridden with a spade bit and a bosal, or hackamore. At first, the rider uses the bosal to show his horse what to do, and during the next year gradually begins using the bridle as each signal comes to mean something to the horse. Then he becomes a bridle horse in the true sense of the word.

Bridles and Curbs

Here on the ranch, I ride nearly all my horses in a browband bridle with a throatlatch so a horse can't rub off his bridle. I might even tie a horse with the bridle reins if I don't pack a halter to the backside of the ranch that particular day. All our horses know how to tie with a bridle, and I can't remember when one has had a problem.

When using a split-ear headstall, be sure the split fits easily around the base of the horse's ear without rubbing.

- Generally, leather curb straps are used on the more advanced, signal-type bits, what you might call "older horse" bridles for more finished horses. Again, rules vary, depending on the competition. In reined cow-horse competition, for example, only a leather curb can be used.

- Anything goes at home, but in the competitive arena, a curb chain must be legal for showing. That's explained in every association rulebook, but generally the curb chain must be at least ½-inch in width and fastened so that the chain is smooth and flat, not twisted.

Bosals and Hackamores

Years ago I broke everything on the New Mexico ranch with a hackamore, and then moved the horses into the snaffle bit. Because I lost time in transitions between the two, I started using a snaffle bit to start my horses. Now, though, I put 3-coming-4-year-olds in a bosal because I can show them at 4 and 5 in hackamore classes at reined cow-horse events. Here are a few things to think about when using a bosal.

- A traditional bosal is made of rawhide and used during the time a young horse's permanent teeth develop, when the mouth is sensitive.

- Bosals come in all sizes and weights, and the goal is to develop a horse that operates in a lightweight bosal, which most horses seem to prefer. Appearances can be deceiving; sometimes a bulky-looking bosal isn't that heavy.

- Although not considered traditional, people make nosebands of all kinds of material and use them like a bosal. A nylon noseband, for example, is lightweight, and horses seem to like it. A horsehair bosal isn't heavy, and a horse is sensitive enough to respond to that. When the horsehair is wet, it stiffens and stays stiff for about a day.

- It's easy to sore a horse's jaw or nose with a bosal. To protect your horse, you might work silicone from the hardware store into a bosal to cover the roughness, or even wrap it in duct tape.

- A bosal works on pressure, not leverage, and there is pressure on the horse in completely different places than those on a snaffle bit. It can be hard to switch between the two because a colt has a hard time understanding what you want at first. It's like starting all over again.

- A novice hackamore horse at first doesn't understand those bosal pressure points at all. If you lift the right rein, he feels pressure on the right side of his nose and on the left side of his chin. So his nose wants to go to left, away from the pressure on his nose, and his chin wants to go right, away from the pressure on his chin. Your horse really can get confused for a while, so work slowly and try to show him what you want. Show your horse the difference between the snaffle bit and the bosal.

A bosal applies pressure in different places than a snaffle bit, so a young horse can be confused at first when changing from one piece of headgear to the other.

Reins, Romals and Mecates

I usually use 8-foot split reins at home. I have romals, too. I don't ride a lot with my romals on the ranch, but I do show quite a bit with a romal. Although I finally bought a real horsehair mecate, mecates weren't used much where I came from in New Mexico. Even my hackamores have two reins on them, not the loop rein with the tie rope.

- Many people prefer split reins and ride with them all their lives. In the versatility trail class, you might have to ground-tie your horse. If you use split reins for that, you don't have to unhook a romal rein or carry a tie rope. Split reins work fine in the other versatility classes, too.

- Romal reins have their place, especially in the versatility western riding class and the cow-horse work. With a romal it's easy to control your horse and keep him gathered with less hand action for the judge to see. With split reins, you must lift your hand high, but with the romal you move only the lower part of your wrist. If you really need to help that

horse during a class, you can pick up the romal reins and elevate him without it being too obvious.

- A horse must neck-rein well and be really light to be ridden with the romal. If you can move your horse's shoulders easily, you probably can do well with a romal. If you must drop your hand and work to move your horse's front end, you probably won't.

- If you ride with split reins at home, you might cheat a little and not realize it, but at the show your horse doesn't ride as well as you thought. With a romal, you learn that at home.

- Use inexpensive romal reins for practice and keep your rawhide romal nice for the show. Get used to the way a romal feels and controls your horse.

- A mecate is like a romal in this respect: If you haven't used a mecate much, try it at home before you go to a show. Otherwise, you feel awkward using it.

Here's a close look at how the romal rein is held in the left hand with the tail in the right.

The tail of the mecate is draped around the saddle horn and then tucked underneath the chap belt.

- The advantage to a mecate: With the single loop rein you tend to ride one-handed more than you do when you use split reins. Using a mecate is like using a roping rein, and you teach your horse to neck-rein without realizing it. That might not be the traditional way, but the end result matters, and your horse learns to neck-rein.

- The mecate loop rein also has another small coil in it, which the rider carries for adjustment. That's a lot to have in hand and takes practice. If it's necessary to let out the loop rein, the small coil can even be dropped.

- Most people use rope mecates, but a horsehair mecate is traditional. A horse feels that prickly hair rein more than he does a rope one.

Cavessons

A cavesson is a great training tool when it's adjusted correctly and used for only a short while. I might use a cavesson underneath the headstall on a horse's fourth or fifth saddle, but seldom for more than 10 rides after that. I don't want to rely on the cavesson as a permanent fix.

- You can use a rope cavesson, leather one or even an English-style figure-eight cavesson. The leather cavesson is good on colts, and the nylon rope cavesson comes later, as a horse matures.

- The cavesson noseband shouldn't be tight, pushing into your horse's skin. Most people ride with one snugged really tight, but set yours with the noseband barely touching your horse all the way around his nose. However, if the

A cavesson is a good short-term training tool, but at some point a horse must learn to pack a bit with his mouth closed.

noseband is completely loose, there's no real point in using a cavesson.

- When you ride with a snaffle bit, make sure the cavesson is high enough that your horse isn't accidentally pinched when you pull on the reins. When a cavesson is set too low, the bit ring can pinch your horse's lip against the cavesson, and he throws his head. To avoid that, set your cavesson about 3 inches above your horse's lip.

- A cavesson only helps a horse learn that he can keep his mouth shut, so use one for about 10 saddles and then take it off

your horse. During an easy ride, don't use the cavesson, but give your horse a chance to learn how to pack his bit and keep his mouth shut. Turn and handle him some. He might open his mouth a little at first, but soon learns to carry his bridle with a quiet mouth.

- You can overuse a cavesson, and the time comes when a horse needs to learn to pack a bridle. If you ride all the time with a cavesson and then take it off, your horse soon opens his mouth again because, by then, he's learned to feel for that cavesson and push on it. So don't ride your horse every day with it.

- Tools like a cavesson or martingale never should become full-time crutches for your training program. If you allow that to happen, when you get to the show pen, where you can't use a crutch, your horse program can fall apart.

Martingales

I seldom use a martingale, usually only when I work a young horse on cattle, and then I use a running martingale instead of a German-style martingale that clips into the little d-rings on the reins. The running martingale is only for support, to help a colt understand what his position should be, and the work is soft and methodical. I back a colt into a turn and pull him through the turn on a slow cow. With that consistently slow, easy work, a colt learns how to position himself to work a cow.

- The big mistake people make with a running martingale is adjusting it too short. If the martingale doesn't immediately pull down the horse's face when the rider picks up the reins, he thinks the martingale is too loose. So he shortens the martingale and pulls again, which only teaches a horse to be hard and tough instead of light and soft.

- A too-tight martingale teaches a horse to push on the bridle. Because the martingale pulls down continually, a horse thinks that lifting his head might bring relief, but he can't get any. So he lifts his head and pushes, which really hinders his training.

A too-short running martingale teaches a horse to become tough and resistant, rather than soft and light. Ideally, the rings should come to or almost to a horse's throatlatch.

Here's an inexpensive, lightweight version of a German martingale, and it's easy to make and use.

- Adjusted as it should be, a running martingale becomes a training tool. The martingale rings should be about 2 inches from your horse's throatlatch to almost all the way to his throat. That allows him to be completely natural. If he throws his head, he puts pressure on himself and soon figures out to put his head back down and find relief. Then the martingale teaches him something.

- A purchased German martingale clips into one of many little d-rings on the bridle reins, and most are expensive to buy. For a poor boy's lightweight version, punch a hole in each bridle rein, partway down the rein from the bit. Then run two small ⅛-inch cords from the center of your horse's chest through the bit rings to the outside. Then run a cord through the hole in each rein. Adjust the martingale there and tie a knot. At your horse's chest, knot the two cords together and fasten them to the cinch ring with a snap. The cords should be adjusted to give your horse a long signal time before any pressure gets to the shank of the bit.

- A martingale or cavesson of any kind is only a tool to help your horse understand what you want him to do; neither is a tool to make him do what you want. There is a distinction. If you use the tool for a week or two, as you should, your horse begins to understand what you want, and you soon should be able to completely quit using the tool. Then you've taught your horse something.

Competitive versatility horses and working ranch horses share similar abilities and attitudes—good guidelines when shopping for your versatility horse.

4

THE RANCH-HORSE IDEAL

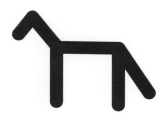

When I think about the perfect ranch-versatility competition horse, I think about the ranch horse I want to ride—a well-broke horse in all respects, one that's light, responsive, maneuverable, athletic and cowy. He has a trainable mind, is a smooth mover, and can move out fast, too, if I need that. The bottom line: My ideal horse for ranch-versatility competition is my ideal horse for punching cows on the ranch.

Riding for arena competition can be so systematic, doing the same things over and over again, that a horse can get bored and dull at his work. That's why I often ride my competition horse to work cattle on the ranch. That freshens his mind, and I still can teach him things—most of the time.

My situation might seem the best of both worlds, but that's not always the case. During ranch work I can't always concentrate on correct maneuvers, but must do what the cattle dictate, whether my horse is in the right place or not. But because of his trainable mind, I also can go right back to my training program and overcome whatever might have been done in a less than desirable way while working cattle.

My ideal ranch horse hasn't changed much through the years, but my understanding about how to get maneuvers out of my horses now is considerably different. Years ago, horses were good, but we didn't have the horse knowledge readily available that we do today. Now training information is easy to

A top ranch-versatility prospect has a trainable mind, a pleasant disposition, and solid conformation.

find—books, videos and clinics. Back then, I learned mostly the hard way, by making mistakes, and fortunately had enough horses to afford a mistake or two.

When you shop for a versatility horse, you don't want someone else's mistake, and if you're lucky, you might find that perfect horse. If you find only a nice-minded, well-broke horse, that's a good start.

The Performance Goal

Any horse you select for ranch-versatility competition must have a brain to deal with the training, a disposition that's pleasant and good conformation to hold up to the work. The importance of the first two is obvious, but even the greatest mind and the best disposition don't mean much if the horse's body can't hold up to his work.

Cost is another thing. You might want a horse that can take you to the show arena now, and a finished horse isn't cheap to buy. But if you can train a horse to do almost anything, you need only a versatility prospect, ideally a mature, broke horse, especially

if you want to compete anytime soon. Otherwise, it could be a year before a young horse is ready for competition.

However, if you're an experienced rider, you can teach a horse some parts of versatility competition although you might need training help for others. Getting a broke, mature horse show-ready when you can do some of the training shouldn't be as costly as a finished horse or as time-consuming as a green horse. Granted, you might have to pay for some training; for most people that's the cattle work, but you probably can pick up some new skills in the process.

Be honest with yourself about your horsemanship skills. Otherwise, your ranch-versatility experience can frustrate you and your horse a lot.

A Broke Horse

A versatility horse is the definition of a broke horse, and that's what I need to compete and win. I can cut a cow on a broke horse, go down the fence, rope cattle, open gates and do whatever, so a versatility horse

Broke horses are matter-of-fact about whatever they're asked to do.

A broke horse meets certain standards, no matter if he's going to work in the pasture, down a trail or into the arena.

is a lot like a using horse on the ranch. First and foremost, I'm a rancher, even if I've been blessed while showing horses. I expect certain things from any horse, no matter if I show him or work cattle at home.

- A broke horse tries to do anything I want, and that is expected of any horse. He can hit a running-walk to move across the pasture or a long-trot to get to the backside, even if he has to trot miles. A broke horse can lope and hold it steady, with loose bridle reins. While he does these things, he watches out for me and for any holes in the ground, no matter if he's going across the ranch or the show arena.

- A broke horse doesn't fight me. He doesn't resist doing what I ask of him, but listens and wants to be my partner. I often work alone because there's so much country to cover. My horse must get me to a cow, work with me to rope it, stay back on the rope so I can get off and treat the cow, and do his job willingly. That's true for any horse I show, too.

- A broke horse is matter-of-fact about his work. It's not just what the horse does, but how he deals with his work. At branding time, for example, my horse might sort 300 to 400 cows off the calves through a gate. He lets the cows by, but holds the calves, and switches back and forth, pushing or holding cattle, but he never gets rattled. That's the point where many horses get rattled and get in too much of a hurry, but a broke ranch horse stays quiet and does his job.

- A broke horse should respond and perform no matter where I am. That same ranch horse should back into a roping box, and most of my ranch horses have been used for arena roping. They're also started on cattle and can cut a cow, some better than others, and every ranch horse here can stop and turn around.

- All the above describes the broke horse you initially need for the versatility class—a solid horse to ride while you learn the event, one that listens to your requests and willingly wants to do those things for you every time you ask.

- It's not easy to find a broke horse, especially if you want one that looks great, too; that's asking for a lot. But more than looks, your versatility horse must have a quiet mind and be tolerant and forgiving when you mess up riding him, which we all do at times.

- The good news: Like any great kid's horse, an experienced, well-broke versatility horse seldom decreases in value. When you're ready to step up to another versatility horse, somebody who needs and wants that seasoned first horse always comes along.

Find Your Partner

Usually people interested in versatility ranch-horse competition typically can ride although they might not have had much opportunity to work cattle. If that describes you, then finding a savvy cow horse should be at the top of your list.

- Look for a decent cow horse. He might not be the best in the world, but should be solid on his cow work, nice-minded and very forgiving. His strong cattle experience can help you develop your cattle skills. Even if this first reliable cow horse can't win the halter class, you can have so much fun learning with him. Then you look for that second, really pretty and, of course, higher-priced horse with more sting.

- You probably can get by even if that first decent cow horse hasn't been shown, for example, in trail. Because he's gentle and has that good mind, he can learn those trail things quickly, and you can enjoy teaching him those skills.

- "Solid" can be a qualified description. Be sure you qualify to ride the solid horse you find. Some horses might be solid, but only for a truly advanced rider or competitor. An advanced horse can fall apart really fast with a novice competitor, and afterward the horse's ability never gets any higher than his rider's.

- Green isn't ideal. Neither horse nor rider improves much if both are green at versatility competition. Likely they

That's hard to do, and the hotter-minded and higher-energy the horse, the harder that becomes, especially for a novice versatility rider who's still learning.

- Typically, a novice versatility rider gives mixed signals with his feet and hands, and his hands can be too fast on the bridle reins. All that makes a nervous horse even more anxious, and he can get on the muscle. An advanced rider can deal with the situation without the horse becoming more excited, but when it comes to typical novice mistakes, an anxious, nervous horse doesn't tolerate or forgive much.

You create a working relationship with your horse simply by spending time with him.

remain at the same skill level and, before long, both become frustrated. A green horse isn't solid enough to carry on through many rider mistakes, especially during the cow work. Plus, a green horse often gets heavy in the bridle and starts jabbing his front feet in the ground when he stops. That's because he gets mixed signals from his green rider, who hasn't been on that first, solid horse to learn what he must know to help a young horse perform well.

- A hot horse only increases the degree of difficulty. That quick, excitable horse with an extremely high energy level can't handle mixed signals from his rider. With so many maneuvers in five versatility classes, a rider must pump up his horse to perform and then relax him several times throughout the day.

It's easier to master new skills with a solid, reliable riding horse that wants to please than it is with a green, high-strung or "hot," high-energy horse.

- A forgiving horse helps overcome confusion. When his rider makes a mistake, this horse's attitude is, "That's okay." Forgiveness comes in many forms, and a reliable, seasoned, mature horse can tolerate and forgive errors, especially those made by a rider trying to learn new skills.

- Find a forgiving horse, not a green, hot or nervous horse. Throughout the day, many things in versatility competition, from lead changes to dragging logs to cow-handling maneuvers, can cause you to lose confidence and points. A quiet, forgiving horse can help handle those problems for you.

- When you find that reliable versatility horse, you can partner up simply by spending time with him. You want to create a working relationship and have your horse's respect, and that takes time and riding.

- Your horse wants to please you, and that's what you want, too. Don't spoil your horse or allow him to get by with things until he has no respect and pushes you around. When he loses his respect for you, he's not your partner, but somebody looking down his nose at you.

- You must be the alpha, the leader, in the relationship with a new horse. If you need help to establish that relationship or to master versatility skills, get it. Ride with a top hand or attend a clinic. Clinics are excellent because you learn how to improve your own skills, and almost everyone must have help at some point.

From Head to Tail

Much of what I like in a horse comes from being a rancher, and a horse must hold up to my day's work. On the big New Mexico ranches we often rode 60 or 70 miles a day. A horse with poor conformation didn't last, and

A trapezoid, formed by a horse's top line and underline, and the angles of the shoulder and hip, gives a horse balance in his conformation and movement.

heavily muscled horses sometimes became fatigued. But any ranch horse must have some width and substance; without those, he can be pulled all over the place when I have to rope and handle cattle.

There is such a variety of horses available, and I truly can't say I dislike any of them because I've ridden really good horses that had everything I don't like in a horse's conformation. Things work that way sometimes. But a horse with a pretty head, thin neck, big, round butt and good bone always catches my eye and appeals to me.

Here are some of my ideas about any horse's conformation. Someone else's ideas might be different.

- With five classes in versatility competition, a horse must be fit to work and structurally correct enough to do his job in the long term. Don't invest your money, time and effort in a horse when he can't hold up physically to the work.

- There isn't a perfect horse, but many are built well, and some conformation flaws are easier to live with than others. A high tail-set, for example, doesn't interfere with a horse's ability to work, but if his leg bones don't line up straight, the horse gets sore and lame and can't do his job.

- Many people who judge a horse's head say you can't ride it, but everyone still wants to see that pretty face and a horse that's wide between those big, soft eyes.

- In most halter classes, a judge checks a mare's or stallion's teeth to see if the horse has an overbite, a parrot-mouth. That isn't a problem with geldings since they aren't breeding stock.

- Some horses have big or long ears, and others have short ones. As long as the ears are in proportion to the horse's body, they're okay.

- A fine, thin throatlatch is really important for bridling a horse, in other words, to help him learn to carry a bit softly with his head on the vertical. A horse that's thick through the throatlatch is hard to bridle up because he can't flex easily there.

- A nice, thin neck should tie in high to a horse's shoulders, and the top line of his neck should be balanced. In other words, for a horse' natural balance, the middle part of his neck should be about even with or maybe even a little higher than his withers. A horse with a too-straight neck coming high out of his withers isn't desirable.

- Typically a horse should have sloping shoulders. Training and performance maneuvers aren't as difficult for a horse with sloping shoulders as they can be for a straight-shouldered horse, even though some straight-shouldered horses perform well.

- A lot of muscling in the V between a horse's front legs, especially inside the forearm, is what a judge wants to see for a halter class. But for performance, a horse heavy there can be too muscle-bound to move his front end well when he pulls a leg to the side during a spin. A horse with less muscling, a little flatter between the front legs, can easily move and maneuver.

- When looking at a horse from the side, a trapezoid is formed by the horse's top line and underline, and the angles of his shoulder and hip. That trapezoid shape gives a horse balance in his conformation and movement. The trapezoid should be correct, with the angle of the hip the same as the angle of the shoulder. The top line should be shorter than the underline, which runs underneath from the girth to the flank.

- It's hard to ride a mutton-withered horse that's round-backed with little to no shape at his withers. There's excess motion under the saddle, and his withers can get sore. When a horse is saddled, the saddle should sit there without the cinch being pulled really tight, which doesn't happen with a mutton-withered horse.

- People want short-backed horses, but sometimes that can get in the way when maneuvering him because a short-backed horse isn't as flexible and can't move as freely as one with a medium-length back. Ideally and for the halter

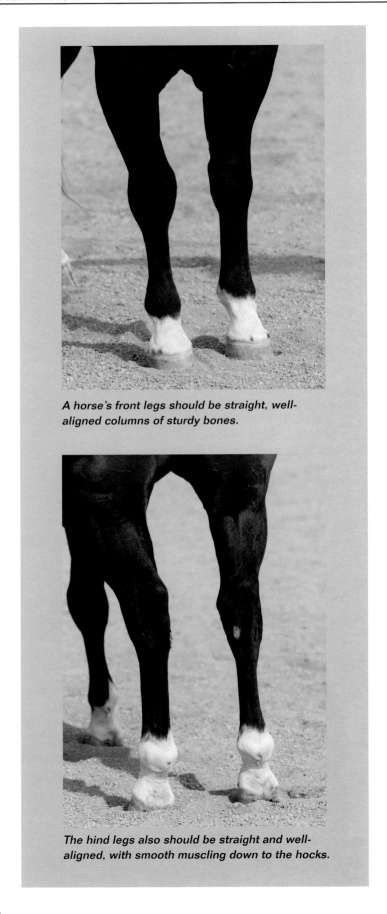

A horse's front legs should be straight, well-aligned columns of sturdy bones.

The hind legs also should be straight and well-aligned, with smooth muscling down to the hocks.

portion of the versatility, the back should be in proportion to the rest of a horse's body. Then no one part of the body gets excess strain.

- A horse should be deep through the heart-girth so he can draw a lot of air when he needs it.

- When seen from behind, a horse should not be wider at the hip than he is down through his stifles and feet. A horse should be correct and fairly square there, with his stifles just as wide as the top of his hip.

- A horse's back end should be well-muscled with the muscling going all the way to his hock, and he should have a smooth tail head. A horse with a short hip, light muscling or high tail head isn't at all pleasing.

- A horse should have substance to his bone, especially in the legs, which should be straight. When a horse's cannon bones don't line up with his knees, he can't last long when he's put to work. The length of a horse's legs and his height is relative. Years ago cowboys had sorting horses and gathering horses. A leggy, rangy gathering horse covered a lot of country, and after the cattle were gathered, the cowboy caught his sorting horse to cut cattle all day. But both horses' legs had substance.

- A horse's knees and hocks should be in line with his column of leg bones and close to the ground because of his short, sturdy cannon bones. Some horses with knees and hocks high off the ground can do many things, but not always.

- A horse should have a medium slope to his pasterns. A pastern that's straight up and down is rough-riding, and horses that are really straight tend to have navicular problems. A horse with long, long sloping pasterns doesn't hold up well in the long run either.

- A horse's foot should be larger, rather than smaller. A 1,200-pound horse shouldn't wear a double-ought shoe in front. If he does, he can't stand up to his work for any length of time.

Halter vs. Performance

A halter horse and a performance horse are two different animals. If the typical halter horse were a performance horse, we'd all ride him. But we don't because a typical performance horse does just that—he performs and usually much better than the halter horse.

A real halter-class horse's shoulders are about as large as his hips. But for a performance horse, I prefer one to have less shoulder and more hip. Because he's not muscled as heavily on the front end as the back, his forehand moves easily. He uses his back end to carry his front end, and it's natural to him. His heavy hindquarters can handle the front-end weight, which means I have to do a lot less training on that type horse; most maneuvers are more natural for him to make.

The problem in ranch-versatility competition: Four of the five classes are performance-oriented, with halter the fifth and final class of the day. A versatility horse is a riding horse, but a judge still looks for a pretty horse in the conformation class. A lot of good-looking horses can perform, but the horse that wins the halter conformation class isn't necessarily the most athletic horse there.

If a horse does well in the performance classes, and a judge really likes the way the horse works and moves, that can help the horse's placing somewhat in the halter class. It really isn't supposed to, but that's human nature. When a judge recognizes a solid performer, even though the horse might not be completely right for the halter class, the judge might give the horse the benefit of the doubt.

If you look for a horse with quality, balanced conformation, he probably can physically handle the versatility performance workload. Any conditioning you do only helps improve his appearance for the halter class.

Four of the five versatility ranch-horse classes are performance events, with the fifth class being a ranch-horse conformation halter-type class.

Although any individual personality quirk might be a consideration when purchasing a horse, a pleasant and respectful manner should not be a negotiable item.

Negotiable or Not

When you reach the point of test-riding a horse for purchase, you have a good idea of the skills you'd like him to have. Some skills might be negotiable, depending on your riding ability, but other skills might not be.

The important thing: Be honest about the skills you're capable of teaching a horse—setting up for the conformation class, for example, or how to approach a trail obstacle. Be equally honest about skills that might be beyond your abilities, such as a 360-degree spin or handling cattle.

Don't forget to check the basic skills any broke horse should have. Horses are individuals, and all have their quirks, but day in and day out, a well-broke horse provides a pleasant, satisfying riding experience.

A broke horse should:

- be easy to approach, catch and halter.

- respectfully keep his distance when you lead him.

- quietly stand tied away from his buddies.

- quietly stand untied while you groom and saddle him.

- be easy to saddle and bridle.

- stand still when you mount and dismount.

- travel consistently in the three basic gaits—walk, trot, and lope.

- understand how to rate his speed.

- give his head quietly for left and right turns without delay.

- stop easily on command and stand still.

- back without great resistance.

- allow you to pick up and handle his feet easily.

- load readily into the trailer and unload.

- accept your guidance and build your confidence.

How well your horse shows in a ranch-versatility conformation class reflects how you handle him when you're afoot at home.

5

GROUNDWORK AND THE RANCH-HORSE CONFORMATION CLASS

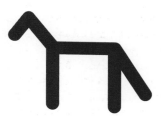

You train or untrain your horse all the time. Anytime you handle him, from the minute you walk into the corral to catch your horse, saddle or ride him, you're training him to do—or not do—what you want. No matter your horse's age, every day what your horse learns, good or bad, depends on what you do with him.

Some people think they should make pets of their horses and always treat them like pets, but that's not necessarily so. When a horse is allowed to be pushy and walk over his handler, problems start, and problems on the ground lead to problems in the saddle.

Other people think being dominant in the relationship with a horse means carrying the biggest stick. This type person only reacts to situations; he overcorrects and misuses his horse because he doesn't know how to fix his horse problems. If he knew, he'd be proactive and show his horse what to do.

Instead of either extreme, you must simply maintain your horse's respect, and you gain his respect with firm, fair and consistent treatment. At times you must be really firm and dominant in the relationship, but that doesn't mean you carry a big stick and take advantage of it.

An arena fence can be a helpful tool when working afoot with a green or a fresh horse.

The best way to prepare your horse for showing is to be consistent in how you handle him. Consistency is important with any horse. Just because he gets things right one day doesn't mean he can the next, or that he might not test you another day. But when you're consistent in what you do, your horse can figure out what you want. That's what doing a good job of handling and riding your horse comes down to—how well and consistently you show him what you want.

That's my philosophy—show my horse what I want, rather than cram a maneuver into him or force him to do one. My consistency in showing him what I want really affects how fast he picks up on the maneuver.

The Performance Goal

When you're afoot handling your horse, you want him to be with you—not pushing or pulling on the lead, but coming with you physically and mentally. You want your horse to be respectful, yet at ease, no matter what you ask him to do.

Groundwork isn't all about preparing for the ranch-versatility conformation class. Groundwork is your preparation for riding, where you learn to read and control your horse before you ever get on him. If he doesn't respect you when you're on the ground, he has no respect when you're in the saddle. Problems afoot with your horse bleed over into your control when you ride.

In the same way, when you're afoot and have your horse's respect, that carries into the saddle with you. What he has learned during your groundwork comes easily when you're in the saddle. When you're afoot, for example, and teach your horse to square his feet each time he stops at home, he knows how to do that for the conformation class, and he's more apt to do that when you ride and stop him. Any time your horse stops and is balanced on his feet, he's ready for whatever comes next. So use your time afoot to prepare your horse not only for the conformation class, but also for when you ride him.

Review Your Skills

Most of the maneuvers below are used in a ranch-versatility conformation class. Although I've never been asked to back my horse in the class, I want to be able to back him if necessary. Granted, I don't always set a horse up perfectly at home, but I do want him in the habit of standing fairly square and balanced whenever I stop him, no matter if I'm afoot or in the saddle.

Your horse probably already does the things below to some extent, but put a halter on him and really evaluate how well he performs.

- Lead your horse at a walk.

- Lead your horse at a trot.

- Stop your horse.

- Set up your horse as if he's in a halter class at a show.

- Turn your horse in each direction.

- Back your horse.

Is he respectful of you and comfortable being with you? Does he respond quickly, or is he slow to react your cues? Is he slow because you should be a little more demanding or because he doesn't understand what you want? Is he too stall-fresh to make a smooth transition, or too leery of you to perform smoothly and easily?

You soon realize how consistently or inconsistently you've been handling your horse afoot. You also probably know what you need to do to prepare him for the conformation class.

At the Walk

When I've ridden a colt several days in the round pen, the sixth or seventh time I try to lead him to the pen, it's, "No. I can't go there." Or I might start to lead him to the barn, and he says, "Nope. I can't go there either because you might saddle and ride me."

Most colts go through that at some point, and that's when I teach a colt to lead up beside me. The same process I use on the colt can work on an old, seasoned horse, too. Consistency is the key. The more consistent I am in doing this exercise, or anything with my horse, the quicker he becomes comfortable and responds.

- Use a well-adjusted halter with a sound lead rope on your horse.

- In your left hand, carry a longe whip, but fold the long tail of it down and hold it in your hand so that the tail doesn't flop

Consistent ground handling is the key to teaching a horse to be respectful and responsive at home and in a versatility conformation class.

around. Or tie a flag on an old fiberglass cattle prod to carry in your left hand.

- Lead your horse on your right between you and a good fence. A barn alley or a fenced lane can work. With the fence, your horse can't get away from you. Without the fence, he learns to swing his

body out and away from you and escape what you want him to do.

- Stand at your horse's shoulder and cue him to move forward. When you cluck or smooch to your horse, tap him on the butt with the longe whip or the flag if necessary. He likely moves forward

67

quickly, but then might stop once he goes past you. Don't worry about that; just lead him down the fence again and ask him to come up beside you again.

- Do the entire process, bringing your horse up beside you, several times. Be consistent and cue him every time before you tap him with your left hand. Usually going down the alley one way and coming back the other is enough to deliver the message, and before long you can step to your horse's shoulder and cue him, and he comes forward right with you.

- Raise your energy when doing this exercise. If you slouch around with your head slumped down, your horse is less

likely to understand what you want. He has a hard time distinguishing which part of your body he needs to move forward with, but he can learn to read your body language. When you stand straight, your horse sees and understands a clear point of reference that tells him he must go forward with you.

At a Trot

Leading a horse at a trot also is part of the ranch conformation class, and I want my horse to transition easily from a walk into the trot when I go past the judge. I teach a horse to trot beside me in the same way he learns about walking alongside me—in the alley, but I'm a little demanding about it when we trot.

Using the fence and the flag helps a horse learn how to make a smooth and straight transition from the walk to the trot.

You might have to be more demanding, too, especially at first, to get your horse to trot freely with you.

- When your horse easily walks beside you in the alley, set him up against the fence just like you did at the walk. This time, use your cue fast as you cluck or smooch him into a trot, and use the flag in your left hand if you must.

- Be more energetic when asking your horse to trot than you are when asking him to come with you at a walk. Again, he learns from your body language. Once your horse understands that it's okay to trot right beside you, getting the trot should become easy.

Lead to Ride

When you work with a colt that's spooky or flighty, leading him at a trot in the round pen can help prepare him for his first ride. Your position near the middle of the horse, whether you're on the ground or on top of him, is what a spooky colt isn't used to seeing. Help him learn that you being there is okay before you get on him.

- In the pen, stand at the colt's shoulder and handle him just as you would alongside the fence. Lead him at a trot around the pen a few times each way until he's comfortable in the different setting.

- When you do get on to ride, the colt should be used to you being in position alongside him. It shouldn't bother him too much to look back and see you out of the corner of his eye when you're in the saddle.

The Stop

"Whoa" means stop. Make clear to your horse that whoa means stop, be still and stand right there—not halfway down the aisle. This holds true in your groundwork for the conformation class and carries into your riding. When you say whoa, you must mean it, no matter if you're on your horse's back or on the ground.

When working along a fence line, a horse can't swing his hindquarters away from the handler to evade making a straight stop.

- The best time to practice stopping and standing still is when your horse is tired after you've ridden him. A fresh horse doesn't want to be still, and you can't blame him because he's ready to do something. But when he's a little tired, he listens and wants to get along with you better than when he's fresh.

- Lead your horse in a straight line. When you ask for the stop, say whoa and then pull down on the lead and a little back toward his chest.

- Don't pull straight back on your horse because a lot of times that only makes your horse push back against the halter.

- Don't pull your horse's head to the side when you stop him. When you do, his butt swings the other way, and the goal is to stop him straight.

- Don't jerk your horse's head when you stop him unless you're in an extreme or dangerous situation. Work toward being smooth and consistent with your cue and the way you handle your lead.

- If your horse wants to "run through" the halter, be more obvious with your cues and body language.

- If you use a nylon or leather strap halter and a stronger cue doesn't result in a good stop, try a rope halter for stopping work. The rope has a little more bite to it than a strap does, and some rope halters have correctional knots along the nosebands.

- When a horse is slow to respond to your stop cue, back him immediately after he finally does stop. Say whoa while he backs to reinforce the correction, and be sure he backs straight. Then immediately walk him forward again, use your cue and stop him.

- If your horse continues to run through the halter, you might put a bridle on him for stopping work. Don't jerk his head; he could start slinging it. Just say whoa and use the bridle to stop him.

- Although you want your horse to stop every time you say whoa, don't always use that voice command as the only cue. Your horse also can learn to stop when you use only the lead, and he can understand both cues.

- When you don't always use the word "whoa" to stop, your horse also learns to read your body language as another cue to stop with you. Don't slouch around.

Give your horse a strong visual cue that it's time to stop.

- Lightness is the goal in your groundwork. When you say whoa and your horse keeps moving, dragging you along, that's disobedience. When he's disobedient, you must take control and gain his respect. Back him off the halter and lead until he's light in hand. That doesn't mean dragging him to a stop or pushing him back; it means he gives a light, soft response when you give a cue or lift on the lead.

- "Whoa" is a cherished word. Your horse must pay attention to it.

Setting-Up

After I've put time and groundwork into preparing a horse for the conformation class, I don't want him to act like he's scared of me when I set him up in the arena. Setting up my horse for a judge comes back to that partnership deal. Because I've worked with my horse, he's learned to trust me, so he stays where I ask him.

When you build that trust with your horse, he works better when you're on the ground and he rides better for you than he does without that trust. Preparation at home helps you create that partnership so you can show your horse at his best in the versatility conformation class.

- Before going to a show, square up your horse at home and see if he looks better set up shorter or longer, in other words, with his front legs and hind legs set closer or farther apart. Decide which position makes your horse look best. That can mean a big difference when the judge looks at your horse.

- Once you figure out how your horse looks best, step off the distance between his front and hind legs. Know that and be able to step it off consistently. At a show, although you might look like you're stepping toward your horse's back end, maybe to straighten a hind foot, you're really checking the distance between his front and hind legs.

- When you set up your horse for halter work, set his back feet first. Lead him

Here, Black Hope Stik is set up too long—not the best way to present a well-built mare to a judge.

In this shot, Hope is set up too short from head to tail, which doesn't show her conformation at its best.

When Hope is set up to show her conformation to advantage, I step off the distance between her front and back legs.

into place, get his back feet even and then move the front feet. That's easy because you stand right there at his front end. At first, pick up and place a foot if you must. Consistency is the key in your horse learning to square his feet and hold the position.

- Once you set up your horse, he might cock a back foot. If you're on his left side, and his right foot is cocked, push his hip to the right to make him stand square, or vice versa. Don't push too hard because your horse could take a step, which you don't want.

- When you consistently square your horse's feet anytime you stop him at home, he learns to do that automatically and it's no big deal when he's at the show. Eventually, your horse wants to stand square because he's in the habit of doing that every day.

The Turn

When I handle a horse on the ground, I want to be able to turn him on his forehand or the hindquarters and in either direction. He already knows how to move his butt away from me and give me his head if I've handled him right catching him. (See "Effective Groundwork.") By now he also should know that a smooch means for him to move in the direction I give him. I can build on those things to get the turns I want. Anybody can.

- When you ask your horse to move his hindquarters, step farther back and to the inside, closer to him and right between his shoulder and his rib cage. If he doesn't step his back end away from you, smooch and use your thumb or the end of your longe whip to bump him in the ribs. Push about where your foot connects with his side to move his hindquarters for a turn on the forehand.

Often in a conformation class, a competitor trots his horse to a cone and then around it, usually to the left.

Eventually, when you step toward his back end, he should turn on his forehand and move his butt away from you.

- Use the same approach to turn your horse on his hindquarters, but stand alongside his neck, between his head and his shoulder. Smooch and then use your thumb on his shoulder, if necessary at first, to move his forehand with his weight on his back end.

- If your horse doesn't respond when you give him direction with your lead rope, your body and your thumb, slap your leg with the tail of the lead rope as you smooch. Do what you need to do to get a response—and don't do all that stuff without getting one. When you ask, your horse should respond.

- Don't forget that you need to work on both sides of your horse. Move his forehand and his hindquarters to both the left and right.

- Teaching your horse to move his forehand and hindquarters helps when your horse sets up crooked in the conformation class. Take a step toward his hindquarters as you smooch, and he should move his back end, or step forward and smooch to move his front end and square his feet.

Backing

Although I've never been asked to back a horse in a conformation class, every horse ought to be able to back. When a horse backs nice and light when I'm on the ground, he usually backs the same way when I'm on him.

Being able to back your horse is a skill you should have no matter if you show, trail ride or do ranch work. When you can back your horse, you can get out of a tight place, and it's no big deal.

- To back your horse, stand at his left with a fence on his other side to help keep your horse straight. Smooch to your horse and pull back at about a 45-degree angle on the lead. If the horse tucks his chin against his chest, pull it up and out and continue to back him straight. If necessary, when you cue for the back,

Anyone should be able to back his horse out of a tight spot even if he's never required to backs a horse in a conformation class.

use your thumb in the center of his chest to send him back. All you want at first is for your horse to take one step back. When he does, release him. Then he's more willing to take a second step and look for that release.

- If your horse is heavy in hand when you back him, at first be a little more forceful with your cue, and use a lot of smooching or clucking or whatever you do. Don't pull more or harder on his head; he only backs crooked.

- If being a little more forceful doesn't lighten your horse when he backs, try raising your hand or snapping your fingers to get his attention. A hand in a horse's face is like a stop sign to him. The next time he stops, he's thinking, "That big hand is fixing to come."

- If your horse still doesn't back lightly, use the tail of the lead toward his front legs to get him moving, but definitely smooch

Conformation Class Showmanship

In the ranch-versatility world, the halter conformation class has the same points possible as the reining or cutting. In competition the riding and cattle classes usually come first so the judge can see how well a horse handles work all day and still respond in a halter class.

In the class you usually lead your horse into the arena and to the judge, who looks at your horse's front end as he walks. When you're even with the judge, he usually steps to the side, and you trot your horse past the judge. A cone might be set ahead, about 30 feet away. You trot to the cone and then around it, almost always to the left. This allows the judge to see your horse as he trots straight away and also from the side.

Then you set up your horse in the line-up however you think he looks best. Always be on the offside from the judge, to give him a clear view of your horse, and try to keep your horse somewhat enthused and alert when the judge is looking.

- Before the show, practice the conformation class at home. See how responsive your horse is and how he handles distractions. Have someone play the judge so you know how well your horse maintains his focus.

- At the show pay attention to the arena dirt where your horse stands. If it isn't smooth, your horse might look like he's stubbed a toe in the ground. If that's the case, smooth the dirt so that your horse stands more flat-footed.

- Your horse might look better carrying his head higher, or could appear better with his head lower. Whichever you choose, try to keep his head there consistently.

- When a horse's neck is stretched out a little, it looks cleaner and thinner. Crinkle a little piece of aluminum foil or plastic wrap, or use a cookie to get your horse to lift his head, stretch his neck and put his ears forward.

- A judge might ask to look at your mare's or stallion's teeth, to see if the horse is parrot-mouthed. Gently pull up your horse's top lip for the judge. Again, handle your horse's lip a few times at home first, so he isn't caught off-guard at the show.

- Smooth your horse's tail down at the dock and try to keep his tail tucked between his hips. His butt usually looks bigger than it is.

- At the end of the day, the hardest thing in the conformation class can be keeping your horse half-way alert, especially when the judge is looking. Give your horse a reason to pick up his head and look alert. Again, crinkle that foil or plastic wrap to get his attention.

- Because your horse is tired by the end of the day, he might stand a little hollow-backed in the con-formation class. Before the judge gets to you, run your thumb down your horse's belly to encour-age him to pick up and round his back. That simple thing helps a lot of horses look better, but try it at home first.

- When showing all day, a young or green horse might refuse to drink and draw up through his flanks, but when he's kept somewhat full throughout the day, he should still look good for the hal-ter class. Between classes keep hay in front of your horse to help him stay bulked up and looking better than he might otherwise. Be sure to remove the hay a little before the cow-horse class, so your horse isn't bloated for that strenuous work.

Smoothing a horse's tail and tucking it between his hips shows his hindquarters to advantage.

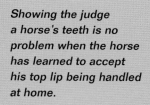

Showing the judge a horse's teeth is no problem when the horse has learned to accept his top lip being handled at home.

first before you do. The next time you ask him to lighten up, your horse thinks that tail might be coming, too. He associates that smooch with moving, and soon you don't have to put any pressure on him to get him to listen to you when he's backing.

Effective Groundwork

Every move you make has an effect on your horse, and you want your horse to respect you instead of run from you or run over you. Here are a few more ways to work effectively when you're on the ground.

- Think about how you approach your horse in the pen or stall. Don't walk too quickly up to your horse. That can startle any horse, especially a young one, and he thinks he needs to get away.

- When you catch your horse, it's important that he move his back end away from you; in other words, he gives you his head. If he throws his butt to you,

Consistent groundwork results in a responsive horse, which makes the daily routine a pleasant experience.

that's when the tail of your lead comes in handy to reposition him.

- When you step into a stall or pen, smooch to your horse and step back, which means, "Turn around here to me." If he doesn't, smooch, pop his butt with the lead and step back. Your horse soon learns that the smooch means to move, and your step back gives him the direction to come headfirst toward you respectfully.

- In the pen, spend a few minutes letting your horse learn to come to you. It might take 10 or 15 minutes for him to learn that's okay. Take the time until your horse wants to come see you and is willing to face you.

- When you turn your horse loose, don't jerk off the bridle and let the bit hit his teeth so that he wants to run away from you. That's training, and it takes about a week for you to undo that. When you turn your horse loose, take a minute or two to let him drop his bit. Rub his head and give him a reason to stay instead of hurrying to leave.

- Working your horse on a longe line is another way to teach him to respect and listen to you, yet not be scared of you. Work him on the line until you can stop him smoothly, send him right or left, and know that he'll trot when you smooch.

- When you saddle and unsaddle your horse, drop the lead or the reins and teach him to be comfortable standing still without being confined. That's groundwork training. It also pays off in the conformation class and in the trail class when you can confidently ground-tie your horse.

- When you groom and saddle your horse, don't walk in front of his head, but walk completely around behind him. If he takes a step, say whoa and step to his hip. That draws his eye from wherever he wants to go and back toward you, discourages him from moving, and helps teach him whoa. Teaching your horse to stand can take time at first, but it's worth the effort.

- Hobble-break your horse. Then he can graze while you eat lunch. If your truck breaks down and you're by yourself, you can hobble him instead of tying him to a barbed-wire fence. Hobble-breaking is just another way of doing groundwork with your horse.

*Build a low-pressure partnership
with your horse.*

6
SOFTNESS AND LIGHTNESS

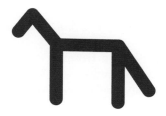

Many riding mistakes result from inexperience, but if you just ride your horse, you do okay. That's the deal: Ride your horse. If you're not comfortable on and familiar with your horse, use your hands and feet to cue him for soft, light responses until doing those things becomes second nature.

When you turn your horse, for example, his rib cage might fall to the outside. When you ride a lot, you don't give his rib cage a thought. You automatically push his ribs back into position and realign his body. But you can't know when his ribs are out of alignment until you spend time riding. That's feel.

You can listen to clinicians and watch videos to help make you conscious of your horsemanship. But more than anything, you must ride to feel what's correct and to develop the timing to fix those things that aren't. When your arms, hands and feet work

together, your horse listens and becomes very manageable. Then you have the control, softness and lightness to do anything with your horse.

So often a horse is unresponsive to the bridle because the rider hangs onto the horse's head so much; the horse simply doesn't feel it anymore when the rider picks up the reins. But every rider can learn how to help his horse be light in the bridle and teach him to flex and soften when he feels a change in the reins. A horse can be light and controlled just off rein pressure. He can feel the weight of the reins move before he feels the bit pressure, and he should respond.

A rider might put quite a few pounds of pull on a shanked bit on a hard-mouthed horse, and the horse still can be pushy and tough. That's because he's never been taught to get off the bridle and find relief

Anybody can learn to help his horse be light and responsive when he feels a change in the reins.

by responding to the pressure, to be soft in hand. He just grits his teeth and pushes back against pressure. A horse that has learned to respond to pressure and look for the release of pressure can be soft in a turn, a stop or any maneuver. Softness and lightness come down to teaching your horse how to respond to pressure, how to find that release.

The Performance Goal

Any maneuver you can do without putting much pressure on your horse benefits your riding program. You have the control to put him anyplace you want at any time, and you and your horse work together. That doesn't just happen. You must develop your horse and teach him that a soft response means the two of you can have a low-pressure partnership.

That partnership is important in every part of the versatility class or any riding situation. No matter what you do, you think about how your horse should respond and know how to maneuver him into giving that response, and he does what you want. He listens to you; he is manageable and maneuverable.

Lightening your horse's response is essential for the ranch versatility class and lays the groundwork for all maneuvers, even trotting across the pen with your horse on a cow. When the cow stops, you pick up the rein, and the horse's back end hits the ground. When your hand comes across his neck, he goes the other way because you've taught him to move his front end. You've already shown him what you expect of him before you ever put him on the cow, so he knows how to respond softly and lightly.

Review Your Skills

Especially when I haven't ridden a horse for a few days, and even on a daily basis, I spend about 15 minutes warming up my horse to be sure he's listening to me. I want to feel life in the reins and know he gives softly to any pressure before I ever ask him to perform an advanced maneuver. So I first refresh his memory about the response I want by flexing and suppling him with some of the exercises from this chapter and those that follow. That's insurance that my horse stays light.

The basic skills described in this chapter help you develop your horse's lateral softness and a soft frame. You then use those skills to develop the body control described in

the next chapter. That body control, in turn, becomes a building block for more maneuvers in the following chapter, and so forth. A review list of skills, along with chapter references, is included at the end of the book.

As you and your horse progress to advanced maneuvers, continue to use the basic exercises as part of your warm-up so you have an idea about how attentive your horse is each day. If your horse feels stiff when you warm up, or his response isn't as light as you'd like, work right there to get that soft response before you move on to the next step. Build that foundation.

Timing and Feel

Timing and feel intertwine and are such important things. Timing is a state of mind, knowing when to put pressure on a horse—or not. Good timing in training is one of the biggest virtues to develop when you work with a horse. Your training is effective, and it takes less time to accomplish your goals because you understand the right time to ask your horse to do a maneuver. Feel is knowing where all your horse's body parts are at all times, and if they are in the correct position for whatever maneuver you ask your horse to perform.

- When you ride, try to figure out your horse's state of mind. The better you learn to read him, the better you can train because you can better figure out when it's time to put pressure on him.

- When your horse is fresh or anxious, don't work on something like spins right then; he's too antsy. Get him moving and take off that edge. A horse that's a little tired thinks a lot more than a fresh horse, who thinks all his movement is "go, go." He soon realizes that he can't and must do something different. That's when a fresh horse starts listening.

- When your horse isn't listening, lope circles—and more than a couple of them. It takes more exercise than that for a horse to even start thinking. Spend a few minutes getting your horse's mind ready for those maneuvers you want to perform.

- Don't just ask your horse to do something; use good timing about when you ask him

Part of having a feel for a horse is realizing when one is too fresh to train, and part of good timing is waiting until the edge is off before the training begins.

for a maneuver. That's important. As you pay more attention to timing, the better you learn when it's easiest for your horse to perform a maneuver and when you can ask more of him.

• Timing affects everything you do with your horse. The best way to help your horse figure out what you want and become soft and light is to be consistent with your timing and feel.

When the head is down and the horse breaks easily through the poll and neck, a horse is really soft and light in hand.

Lateral Softness

Before I ask a horse to flex at the poll and frame his body, I want him to give his head to the left and right. Teaching him to give his head laterally lays the groundwork for him to later flex and give at the poll when I lift my rein hand. Then he's what I call soft in the face and able to drive off his hindquarters.

Teaching a horse to stay off the bridle, the bit, is the start to everything in any performance horse. Only when a horse understands how to flex his head laterally can he learn to flex it vertically and stay off the bit. Teaching those things isn't difficult to do. Again, when you are more consistent in what you do, the quicker your horse figures out what you want him to do.

- A snaffle bit is best to use when teaching most horses to flex laterally.

- For an old veteran extremely heavy in hand, a short-shanked bit with a snaffle mouthpiece, but no curb strap or chain, sometimes works better than a snaffle to achieve a soft response. It's best to first test and use a bit with no curb in a confined area.

- Using a snaffle, first flex your horse right and left while he stands still. You can flex him later at a walk or trot, but if you start there, your horse has to maintain his forward motion and give his face. That's teaching two things at once, and makes it hard for him to learn. So flex him laterally first and add forward motion to your program later.

- "Hinge" or flex your horse laterally by picking up one rein to tip his nose, for example, to the right. Hold that pressure until your horse softens and quits pushing against your hold. When he gives to your pressure, don't keep taking from him. Instead, let him have his relief. Do this consistently. It's almost as if your horse learns to follow the pressure with his nose because the pressure leads him to the release.

- Ask your horse to flex laterally to both the left and the right. Your goal is for him to be equally soft in both directions.

- Only after your horse gives his head easily and softly in either direction while he's standing still should you ask him to flex laterally while walking forward. When you do, establish forward motion first, and then ask him to flex his head 45 degrees to the side. When he does, hold him until he relaxes there, and don't take away the relief he has found by pulling more on the reins. Once he's relaxed, release his head and let him walk forward a few strides before asking him to flex laterally in the other direction.

- Be sure your horse understands what you want when you flex him at a walk. If he seems confused, stop and flex him to the right and left again while he's standing still. Then, walk forward again and ask for lateral flexion. By now, your horse knows how to flex laterally and understands forward motion. Be patient and let him figure out that he can do both at the same time. With forward motion, flex your horse only at a 45-degree angle, not a 90-degree one.

- Later you can flex your horse laterally in a trot or even a lope, but don't go faster than a trot until your horse really understands and becomes very soft in hand. Only then can you use his lateral flexion as a foundation for more advanced things and be successful.

A Soft Frame

When I talk about framing up a horse, I want him to gather and collect his body from his head to his tail, be soft through the poll, and round his back, his spine. Then it's easy for him to perform any advanced maneuver I need on the ranch or in a versatility class.

When a horse isn't in frame, his spine is low and flat. When he moves from that flat position, a horse is very heavy on his forehand, which doesn't work to advantage when asking for a transition or any maneuver. A flat horse can't drive himself forward from the hind end; he can drive off his hindquarters only when his back is soft and rounded.

You might not always realize when your horse's back gets flat, but you can teach him how to soften his body into a good frame. Then he's collected and balanced to perform; he can stop a cow or work around an obstacle. There's no limit to what a collected horse can do, and that's what framing up a horse is all about.

- Don't work on framing your horse's body until he understands how to flex his head to the right and left and give to your rein pressure.

- First learn to frame your horse at a standstill. Later you can put him in frame when he's moving, and that helps

A horse almost needs to be a little behind the vertical when going slowly so that when you pick up speed, he remains on the vertical when traveling fast.

you learn how to position him for many versatility class maneuvers.

- To teach your horse to soften at the poll, begin with him standing still. With both hands, lift your reins up and back, about waist-high. Hold steady there until your horse responds, which can take some time at first. Don't jerk on the bit, just hold. When your horse responds, he softens through the poll to get away from the bit pressure, and drops his nose. Release him immediately, especially when he's first learning what you want.

- Again, don't jerk the bit. If necessary, hold steady and drive your horse into the bit by bumping his sides with both your legs. Your legs are what bring

softness to your horse. When he gives to the pressure and frames his body, stop bumping with your legs.

- To help a young horse figure out what you want and learn to drop his nose, if necessary, you might seesaw the reins. Again, release as soon as the horse softens in your hands.

- When you're consistent with your horse, eventually the lift of your hands and that little bit of leg pressure bring his body into frame, and he's positioned for any versatility maneuver, from side-passing to a sliding stop. When you squeeze your legs to frame your horse's body and keep him in position, his spine rounds, rather than staying low and flat.

- If your horse doesn't soften at the poll and frame up when you pick up on the reins and squeeze your legs, hold him with the reins and kick right at the front cinch until he gives softness. Don't jerk the reins, just hold, and drive your horse into the bridle with your legs.

- If you correct your horse with only your hands, he might get soft at the poll, but he hasn't really learned to be soft in frame. For him to learn that, you must use your legs. Pick up the reins and, when necessary, drive your horse forward into the bridle with your feet until his back rounds and his poll softens.

- You must frame your horse with one hand on the reins at a show, so that slight lift of the reins and the squeeze with your legs become the cues you use in the arena. You might have to reinforce those cues at home, really bumping with your legs and holding or blocking your horse with the bit to remind him what the cues mean and keep his response sharp.

- When you release every time your horse comes to you, he learns to look for that release. But sooner or later he might push against your hands, wanting that release right then. That's when you don't necessarily release him immediately. Instead, hold him in that framed position a few seconds longer, but do this only when your horse really understands what your cues mean.

- Before long, you can ask your horse to frame his body while he's moving. A good place to ask him to hold that frame for a stride or two is when you ride across the pasture. At first, don't expect him to hold his frame all day, just for a few strides each time you ask.

Soften the Heavy Horse

Ideally, a horse should never learn to push on the bridle. When he never learns how to do that, being heavy in hand isn't a problem. Usually a horse pushes on the bridle just a little bit at first, and you might not even notice it. But three weeks later, the horse is heavy in your hands because he's learned how to push against the bit, instead of responding properly to the pressure.

Some horses learn to push on a bridle just trying to survive a rider's pulling and jerking. But no matter the reason a horse is heavy, most people automatically think about using a heavier bit to achieve lightness, and most of the time that's the wrong direction to go.

A horse learns to be heavy in hand, and he can learn to be soft and light. You must teach your horse to be light and responsive, whatever bit is in his mouth. Whether your horse learns to be heavy or light is in your hands. Dealing with a heavy horse comes down to reading the horse and really trying to understand his problem.

- The answer for a heavy horse is seldom going to a bigger bridle, a heavier bit. Granted, with a curb and shanks on a bit, there is leverage; a pound of pull might mean a 3-pound pull in the horse's mouth. But the horse still feels your pull on the reins first and can learn to respond to that initial movement.

- If your horse sulls when you ask him to perform or flips his head when you pull on the bridle reins, the first thing to check is his mouth. Often there are hooks in his mouth or a wolf tooth needs pulling. He might sull because the pain is so great, and he has no other way out.

- When a horse learns to be heavy in hand, even though he's ridden in a shanked bit, take him back to an 0- or D-ring snaffle bit and, if necessary, one with a twisted-wire mouthpiece. A heavy horse can learn to be light when you ride him in a snaffle and frame and gather him up as described in the previous section. Push him into his bridle with your legs and hold him with the reins until he finally finds that place for relief all by himself. Keep bumping with your legs until your horse gives his face; then quit bumping.

- Don't pull hard on a heavy horse's face; just pick up your reins and hold. Make a barrier of sorts for him to bump against when you drive him with your legs. Let your horse find that barrier and figure out how to find his relief.

The hands pick up and hold the reins to create barriers and open doors, and the legs push the horse forward into dealing with those things and figuring out the correct response.

- You can frame your horse and ride him forward, framing him the same way even though your hands move somewhat. As you ride, hold the same pressure until your horse softens and gives. He finally learns and understands that when he gives to the pressure, you don't pull or jerk on his mouth.

- Your feet really are what make any horse lighten up and get off the bridle. Your hands create the barrier, but your legs push that horse forward into dealing with the barrier.

- Usually when a rider continually pulls or jerks on a horse's mouth, the horse doesn't see the point of giving and soon starts fighting back. Then the rider pulls harder, and the horse soon tries to hide his face, right against his chest. Then the rider has nothing—no power-steering, no brakes. The horse has learned to hide his head behind the vertical, and the rider taught him to do that.

- You can get your horse so broke when flexing at the poll that he tucks his nose down and behind the vertical. When that happens, move your hands up and over the top of your horse's head and pick up his face, bringing his nose out and away from his chest.

- You don't want your horse to break a lot at the withers, more than he does at the poll. Your horse should be soft from his poll to his tail, not just soft at the poll or at the withers. Again, move your hands forward and lift the reins over the horse's neck and shoulders to correct his break-over at the withers. Do whatever you must do for your horse to remain light and stay balanced.

Lighten Up

Some horses naturally are light, but even a heavy horse can change and become light, and that's what I see most often at my clinics. Everyone thinks his horse is fairly responsive until we do the following exercise, and a rider usually is surprised to realize how heavy in hand his horse really is.

No matter what I do with a horse at home or a show, I come back to this exercise from time to time. It keeps any horse's response quick, soft and light when I pick up the reins.

- When doing this exercise, your hands should be short enough on the reins that you can pull a rein back to your hip and rest your hand there so it doesn't move. If your hand moves, that can send your horse mixed signals.

- Walk your horse in a 20-foot circle to the left, for example, and ask him to flex and give his face right, to the outside of the circle. As you do, take off any pressure for forward motion and pull your horse to the outside with the right rein and into a stop. Hold him there until he gives his face in response to the rein pressure and immediately release him. After the release, stand quietly a minute and then walk your horse right back into the circle to the right. Do that three or four times and then flex your horse down to a stop in the other direction.

- Your horse shouldn't pull against your hand, but respond quickly to the rein pressure. When you pick up your right hand to flex his face to the side, take slack out of the reins to put pressure on your horse. If his face doesn't come to the right, don't jerk his head, but do somewhat forcefully pull his face to the side, with your hand going back to your hip promptly.

- When you go to the hip with your rein hand, don't pull slowly. Take your hand immediately back to your hip. Don't jerk your horse's head, but tell him to give it to you now. He needs to know that when he doesn't flex and give, there's a consequence.

- If you must hold your horse's head to the side until he gives slack in the rein and relaxes, keep your hand still at your hip. Your horse might walk in circles for a minute or two before he finally figures out to give his face. A stiff, rigid horse might turn around in circles for five minutes. Sit there and hold him. With your hand steady against your hip or upper thigh, you can hold without bumping the horse's mouth, which signals him to move.

- Always flex your horse to the outside of the circle. If you take his face to the inside, his hip goes to the outside, and he doesn't learn to use his back legs to keep his balance. Don't let him disengage his hip like you might do with a colt. In taking the face to the outside, you teach your horse to be soft on the front end, yet keep his weight on his back end. That helps your stops and other maneuvers.

- Teach your horse to be light in the circle and then on a straight line, where his back end must really get into the ground. Then he learns to use his back end and to give his face, and to do both, he must stay light on his front end. When a horse braces on his front feet, he usually pulls against the bridle reins, but when his face is to the side, he really can't brace with his feet.

- When your horse gives his face consistently, occasionally let him come through that turn to the outside, moving his front end around to walk the circle the other way. After he understands what you want, bump him with the calf of your outside leg as he starts turning, but don't use your spur. The bump starts teaching your horse to move off your leg. As he turns, he also learns to step one front leg across the other, to be soft in

A horse needs to know there's a consequence for not flexing and giving a soft response to the bridle rein.

a turn without being scared, to hold his back end in place and to keep his front end elevated—the foundation for your spins. Consistent, quiet work here means smooth, solid spins later.

• You also can use this exercise to lighten up a finished horse before you show him. The exercise helps him understand to

keep his face to the inside of a turn when you ride one-handed.

• When your horse's response is soft at a walk, trot a big circle and flex him to the outside. Don't tense when you do, but stay soft and loose in the saddle. Like before, take out the slack to flex him, and go to your hip. All you really ask your horse to do, at this point, is set his butt in the ground and give you his face. If that doesn't happen at the trot, go back and work at the walk.

- You can progress to do this pull-to-the-hip exercise in a lope after your horse understands what to do at a walk and trot. Lope your horse in a circle; then pick up the rein to move him outside the circle. If he pushes against the bridle, go to your hip and flex him down right then. You might have to do that two or three times in that first session, but about the fourth time, your horse is right there with you, responsive and light.

- An important thing you accomplish: Your horse becomes more responsive without you pulling straight back on his head, which often leads to resistance.

- Another important thing this pull-to-the-hip maneuver accomplishes: That horse learns to stop and wait for your signal about what to do next.

- Pulling the bridle rein immediately to your hip isn't being mean to your horse, but does teach him to be attentive.

Mean is when a rider lopes circles and expects a light response, but hasn't laid the groundwork for it at a walk and trot. That's isn't at all fair to the horse and adds nothing to your riding program.

- Your horse learns to be attentive because you build the response you want. After he understands, but doesn't respond when you lift a rein, flex him down, even in a lope. The ride might be a little rough at first, but he remembers to come to you when you pick up the reins.

- A horse tends to get heavier in hand with faster speeds. He can lope slowly and be soft, but add speed, and he usually gets pushy in the bridle. His back flattens, and it's hard for him to stay gathered. Occasionally pick up the speed to check your horse's response and, if necessary, teach him to stay light as you gain speed.

- This exercise is also great to use on the days you condition your horse. You can keep him very responsive without burning him out on maneuvers like spins or stops. Once your horse has learned such maneuvers, it all comes down to keeping him responsive and in condition.

*Developing body control gives a horse
a way to read his rider.*

7

BODY CONTROL

A horse that's soft and light in hand can be so willing to take his rider's direction. But that willingness doesn't mean a thing when the horse doesn't understand the directions to move his body that his rider gives. That's why developing body control is important with any horse, not just a versatility horse. Working on body control is how a horse learns to read his rider and understand that a particular cue means to do a specific thing and that another signal tells him something altogether different.

There is no possible way to prepare your horse for every specific situation he might experience in the cutting or cow-working portions of a versatility class, let alone the entire competition. But your horse can learn how to take your direction and move his body on cue in a given, specific way. Then it does not matter what the two of you might face. You can communicate and deal with the situation. That is what a versatility class is all about—dealing with different situations.

The Performance Goal

In developing body control you take charge of your horse's forehand, his hindquarters and his rib cage. You learn to direct these parts of his body individually and in unison. When he understands and accepts your direction, the two of you can use these body-control tools to communicate and change leads, fence a cow, open a gate, or do anything necessary at home or in competition.

Body control is such an important horsemanship tool, but it doesn't happen overnight. You must ask your horse to move these different body parts and spend whatever time necessary for him to figure out your cues and learn what he must do in response.

Developing control over your horse's shoulders, hips and ribs is as much about having a maneuverable horse as showing in a versatility class. When you can control your horse's body, you benefit, and it doesn't matter what your favorite horse sport is. If you rope, you can set your horse's hindquarters

It's well worth the time it takes to develop body control because that's such an important tool in anybody's horsemanship program.

and forehand precisely in the box. If you're a barrel racer, you can pick up your horse's shoulder to keep from hitting a barrel. On a trail ride, you can shape his rib cage around the tree instead of hitting it with your knee. Body control isn't event-specific; it's part of good horsemanship.

Review Your Skills

My horse develops the body control and softness he needs to be my partner at the ranch or in the show pen because the little things I do when flexing and suppling him are the foundation for the big maneuvers I want him to perform later.

You can develop that control in your horse by using the previous chapter's exercises as part of your warm-up for things here. Later,

these new exercises become more warm-up tools for checking your horse's response. With them, you build the softness, lightness and body control you need to direct your horse through any maneuver. Refer to the "Review Your Skills" list at the end of the book.

Move the Forehand

I start teaching a horse to move his forehand when he's young and green, but any age horse can learn to do this. Controlling the front end means I can pick up on and move my horse's face, or head, and his shoulders. When I do those things, his neck usually is right where it should be. When I have the control to move his shoulders out of his way, he can work off his back end and always can achieve a better performance.

Lateral flexion is a basic step to gaining control of a horse's shoulders and moving the forehand.

You can improve almost any maneuver your horse performs by learning to control his shoulders. The following guidelines apply to all the forehand-control exercises later in this chapter.

- Use a snaffle bit when working your horse to develop control of his forehand.

- The key to gaining control of your horse's body is to build one step at a time. Get that first step, and the next step isn't so hard to accomplish. If you jump ahead, things don't work too well.

- Shoulder control starts with being able to control your horse's face. He should be comfortable with the lateral flexion in Chapter 6 before you ask for shoulder control. If he isn't and you try the forehand exercises, your horse can get tight and antsy, so first be sure he's comfortable moving forward and giving his head to either rein.

- Move your horse's shoulders at a walk and then a trot until your horse is totally comfortable with combining forward motion and shoulder movement. Then make these shoulder exercises part of your warm-up routine to maintain a soft response. Although some exercises can be performed later at a lope, a lope typically is too fast for learning new maneuvers.

- Be sure to move your horse's shoulders to the right and the left, so you have control in each direction.

- In the exercises, you might pick up the right bridle rein, for example, to move your horse's shoulders left. Ideally the right rein shouldn't touch his neck. If you make a habit of that now, when you ride one-handed later and the rein touches your horse's neck, he might be confused about what you want—a left turn with his head left or moving left with his head and body arced right. Let that rein touch his neck to help him only in moderation and only when your horse has a hard time understanding what you want.

Moving a horse's shoulders on and off the arc of the circle encourages a horse to elevate the shoulders and soften the rib cage.

On and Off the Circle

Use this exercise to check your horse's willingness to elevate his shoulders and to teach him how to do that. The exercise also teaches him about leg pressure and helps soften his rib cage. Used as a warm-up exercise, you can check your horse's response when you ask for his face and shoulders before moving to advanced maneuvers.

- Walk your horse in about an 8-foot, right-hand circle. As he walks, tip his nose only slightly to the right. Then with your right hand in front of the saddle horn, lift the rein straight up and move it to the left to take his shoulders to the left.

- When you pick up the right rein and direct your horse's shoulders to the left, ideally he should take a step or two to the left, off the arc of the circle, and his rib cage should feel soft under your right leg.

- At first, your horse might think you're stopping him. If necessary to keep forward motion, bump him lightly with your right leg. Don't be aggressive, kicking and spurring. Bump just enough to keep him moving.

- If your horse's side is rigid under your leg, bump lightly with your inside foot as you pick up his nose just a bit more to soften his rib cage.

- Reverse the cues to work your horse in the other direction. Ride in a left-hand circle and move your horse's shoulders to the right.

The Figure Eight

When your horse understands how to move his shoulders on and off the circle, change your path of travel. Walk or trot him in figure eights, moving his shoulders, until he's comfortable doing that wherever he goes.

- As you ride around the eight, continue to lift your horse's shoulders and move them on and off circle, just as you did before. The only thing that really changes from the first exercise is your horse's path of travel.

- Soon your horse learns to change his path while elevating his shoulders, and to do that in a steady, consistent manner. This basic step helps so much later when you change leads.

Counterbend the Figure Eight

You can increase the degree of difficulty in the previous exercise by counterbending your horse around the circles in the figure-eight pattern.

- Shape your horse to the right, for example, along the arc of the circle, with his nose to the inside, just as you did before in the previous figure-eight exercise.

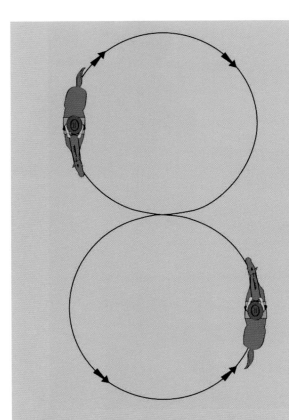

In the figure-eight exercise, the horse's shoulders continue to move on and off the arc of the circle, and all that changes is the horse's path of travel.

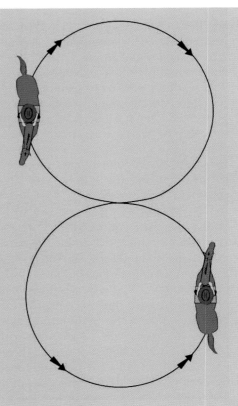

When a horse counterbends his body to the outside while traveling in a figure eight, he learns to cross one front leg over the other—a basic step in learning the spin.

- As you approach the center of the eight, where the two circles join, continue to hold your horse in frame to the right. Then elevate his shoulders, bringing your inside right hand to the left as you direct your horse's path onto the left-hand circle. Although his neck is shaped to the right, his shoulders move to the left as his path of travel changes.

- This exercise teaches your horse to cross one front leg over the other—the first step in a rollback or spin. He learns how to handle his feet and legs without hitting himself, which makes it easy later to teach him those advanced maneuvers.

The Serpentine

The serpentine is a series of half-circles, alternating from left to right, somewhat like a pole-bending pattern, which allows for forward motion. In the serpentine, the horse travels a straight line between the half-circles or arcs.

- Begin by walking or trotting your horse in a straight line. Then bring the right rein across his neck to the left to elevate and move his shoulders to the left, pushing them the opposite way his head and neck are turned. Travel a few strides with your horse holding his body in that arc when you first do this.

- Now ask your horse to travel straight for a few strides before you bring the left rein across his neck to push his shoulder to the right. Then travel straight again.

- Each time you pick up and move your horse's shoulders, his rib cage must move, too, and should be soft under your leg as he travels in frame.

- If necessary, to maintain forward motion, bump your horse at the cinch with your right leg as you push him to the left, or vice versa.

- Your horse should give soft vertical flexion at the poll each time he travels straight after being flexed laterally. At first you might have to ride straight for a distance until your horse understands what you want.

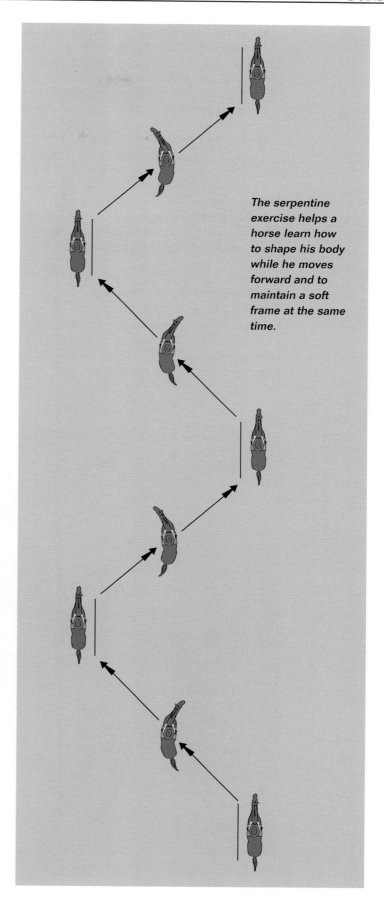

The serpentine exercise helps a horse learn how to shape his body while he moves forward and to maintain a soft frame at the same time.

- As you go straight, don't use both bridle reins hard; you end up playing tug-of-war, and the horse usually wins. Instead, bring your hands in front of your swells or a little higher. Then bump slightly on one rein with your little finger and then on the other rein and bump with both feet until your horse softens and frames his body on the straight line.

- If necessary, go back to the framing-up exercise in Chapter 6 to soften your horse's response. Be sure he first travels in frame before you ask him to shape his body on the arc and hold the frame.

Figure-Eight Back-Through

Traveling in reverse and backing your horse through a figure eight is another way to develop shoulder control. You also move your horse's hip a little as you go, as well as keep him soft through the poll.

- First, back your horse a few steps. Bump with your legs to make him get soft and to make his feet move. Then use your right hand to push his shoulder left as you back him in a right-hand circle. His rib cage should be soft as he shapes along the arc of the circle.

- Bump and release the reins as you back instead of using a steady pull. A steady pull here often creates resistance. Again, use your legs to make your horse soft and get his feet to move.

- When your circle is complete, back your horse straight a step or two, and keep him in frame with his back softly rounded. Be consistent about that.

- Now back your horse the other direction around the eight. With your left rein, push his shoulders right as you back into a left-hand circle.

Backing a horse through a figure eight is another way to encourage a soft response when developing shoulder and hip control.

Flex Around the Circle

Your horse must be fairly decent at the previous maneuvers before you flex him around a circle at a lope. But later, in an advanced maneuver, like a lead change, he's not the least bit worried about giving his head and shoulders, no matter his speed.

- Don't try this exercise until your horse flexes his head easily at a 45-degree angle to the right and the left in a walk and trot, as described in the previous chapter's exercises.

- First, lope your horse on the left lead in a large circle about half the size of an arena. Pick up the left rein to flex his head and nose inside the circle, a little more so than you normally would. Ideally, your horse should willingly give you his nose for four or five strides, and as he does, keep him traveling along the arc of the circle.

- Release your horse from the flexed position and let him reshape his body along the arc of the circle and travel as he normally would.

- Now ask your horse to flex his nose to the right, outside the circle for several strides before returning to the arc of the circle. Be patient and give him time to understand what you want.

- The same as with the serpentine drill, the strides between the flexed positions are important. Your horse should be soft in the poll when he lopes on the arc of the circle between the flexes.

When flexing a loping horse's head to the inside and outside of a circle, keeping the poll soft throughout the entire exercise helps lay the foundation for a smooth lead change.

- If your horse is stiff through the poll, use your little fingers to slightly seesaw the reins as described in the serpentine. Again, if necessary, go back to the flexing and framing exercises in the previous chapter. When your horse responds well, try to flex him around the circle again.

Move the Hindquarters

Controlling a horse's shoulder is only part of the foundation my horse needs for advanced maneuvers in the versatility class or here on the ranch. It's good that he understands about elevating his shoulders, but if he doesn't also understand about moving his hips, I'm just spinning my wheels when it comes to progressing my horse and my horsemanship. When my horse understands how to move his hips in either direction and elevate his shoulders, anything's possible.

Lead changes, for example, seem to be a problem for many people. When you have shoulder control and can move your horse's back end at a lope, you have the foundation to make that change.

A fence is a good training tool when first teaching a horse to move his hindquarters.

Use the tips below when you work at teaching your horse hindquarter control.

- The main thing about moving your horse's hip is that he can become aggravated quickly and might try to wring his tail. If he doesn't understand or is bothered, give him a break and do something else. You can come back to the hip later or even the next day, but don't keep pushing your horse when he's tense and aggravated.

- Whenever your horse gives the slightest response to your cue and tries to move his hip, take off the pressure.

- Use forward motion when you teach your horse to move his hip. Nothing aggravates a horse worse than standing still and being asked to move his hip. In the beginning he doesn't know what you want and usually moves both his front and back ends.

Move Down the Fence

Walk your horse down a fence line, for example, on your right, to teach him to move his hip to the left, or vice versa. Set up things to make it easy for your horse to figure out what you want—control of his hindquarters.

- Put your horse about a foot from the fence to your right. Pick up the reins slightly to gather your horse and elevate his forehand. Maintain forward motion and bump his hip left, toward the inside of the pen, with your outside, or right, leg. When your horse gives any response at all, even a shift of his weight, quit and walk down the fence until he's settled before you ask him to move his hip again to the inside.

- Eventually you want to pick up the inside rein and your horse's shoulder, then move his hip to the inside, and have him walk in a line with his body arced toward the inside of the arena. Being able to do that makes a really nice canter departure and lead change whenever and wherever you want.

- Bump farther back on your horse's side, more toward his hip, and with the side of your foot, not a spur. His side is a touchy area. Your horse doesn't understand what you want yet, and you don't want to teach him to wring his tail.

- When you want your horse to move his hip to the left, shift your weight to the right, and vice versa. That's what you do when you change leads later. Shifting your weight to the outside frees the horse to maintain his balance. If your weight is to the inside, your horse must catch it with his front foot instead of his inside hind, which is what he needs to do to make a clean lead change.

- Maintaining forward motion lays the groundwork for a lead change. Your horse learns he can move his hip while he's in motion, and that's an important part of changing leads.

- The first few times you try to gather your horse and move his hip, especially a young horse, he might try to come to your leg pressure, rather than move away from it. Be patient.

- At first your horse also might try to put his face to the outside, but can't go far. Physically, the fence blocks his way and mentally, it seems to help a horse grasp the idea of moving away from pressure.

- After you go down the fence and move your horse's hip three or four times, turn him around to the inside of the arena, not toward the fence. That reinforces the idea that his nose shouldn't go into that fence when you pick up a shoulder and move his hip.

- If your horse really has trouble understanding, walk him in a circle to the left, for example, and pick up the reins to block the forward motion. Keep him slightly arced to the left and use your left leg to push his hip to the right, completely around in the other direction. Then walk out the other way. Don't do this often because the horse is arced in the wrong position for a lead change and can learn to drop his rib cage to the outside. But sometimes it's easier for him to understand when you show him what you want in a different way.

When initially moving a horse's hip while trotting or loping, the fence can be a point of reference for the rider and also can give the horse a sense of security.

- If you don't think your horse's response is light when you gather him to move his hip, walk him along the fence and move only his shoulder. Pick up his shoulder a few times with the inside rein before you again ask him to move his hip.

- At first, don't worry too much about your horse's shoulders. They might be a little out of place for a day or two until he understands about moving his hip. Only then can you really work on the shoulders, too.

- After your horse is comfortable moving his hip along the fence, pick up his inside shoulder and ask for his hip. When he responds, let him walk straight a few strides and try that again. If your horse seems bracey and stiff at first, hold his shoulder up until he's comfortable before you move his hip.

- Any time your horse gives a response, even a little one, release and let him relax. That's important. Don't teach your horse to be more on the muscle. Do something else for a few minutes and let him relax and become soft and quiet.

- Remember to work both sides of your horse. With the fence to your left, use cues opposite those above to move your horse's hip to the right.

- You can use the fence a lot to move your horse's hip, but that doesn't mean a lot in one riding session. Maybe work down one side and then the other, then quit for the day if your horse does well. A long session can aggravate a horse, but a little one every day doesn't, and the horse soon gets comfortable with your leg back there moving his hip. When you hurry things, your horse gets tight and nervous.

Faster on the Fence

Before you speed up things when moving your horse's hip, be sure he understands what you want. If he doesn't understand how to move his hips at a walk, don't try to move them at a trot.

- When you step up to a faster speed, your horse needs that fence line, which provides a bit of security for him.

- When you teach your horse to move his hips at a trot, do just like you did at the walk. Trot along a fence line, pick up his shoulder and then move his hip.

- Don't increase your speed to a lope until your horse is totally comfortable moving his hips at a trot. Then use the same steps and ask him to move his hips at a lope. Any time he doesn't seem to understand, go back to the trot.

In the Circle

When you first take your horse away from the security of the fence to ask for his hip, trot him in about a 75-foot circle and ask him to flex his head in each direction, like he's already learned to do. Don't ask your horse to move his hip until he's totally comfortable flexing his head at a 45-degree angle each way in the circle.

- If it's tough to get your horse to flex his head softly to each side at a slow jog, walk circles and flex him until he responds softly. Then move to the trot. Don't jump ahead and ask for your horse's hip until you have soft lateral flexion.

- When your horse flexes his neck easily, trot a left-hand circle and ask for his hip. Pick up his left shoulder to arc his face to the left, and use your right leg to push his hip to the left.

- Now trot a right-hand circle and use the opposite cues. When your horse can be soft laterally with his face and move his hip comfortably in either direction—without being antsy—he's prepared to change leads.

- Again, anytime your horse seems aggravated, give him a break. Trot or lope a circle without doing anything. You want your horse comfortable when he flexes his head, elevates his shoulders and moves his hips, so take time to make sure he is.

It's difficult at first for a horse to travel in a circle and move both the shoulder and the hip to the inside, but doing so develops smooth canter departures and lead changes.

In the Open

When I work on this exercise in my arena at home, I sometimes ride diagonally across the pen from one corner to the other. It really doesn't matter where I move my horse's hip in the open as long as I pay attention and keep him headed in a straight line. That's the hard part.

- When you move your horse's hip, look ahead, toward where you want to go. If you don't, it's hard to keep your horse on track in the straight line and move his hip, too.

- Trot across the arena or down it with your horse traveling straight. Look at a specific spot to keep your horse on that straight line. Position his head and shoulders and then move his hip to one side. As soon as your horse's hip moves, release him and go straight again. That's his reward.

- Don't hold your horse's hip to the side a long time. That's hard for a horse and punishes him. He can get to the point he doesn't want to move at all. When you reward him and release quickly, your horse learns to and wants to move his hip all the faster to get that release.

- At first, your horse might go more sideways than straight to the spot, but that's okay as long as he's headed to the spot and moves his hips.

- Again, before you increase your horse's speed to a lope in this exercise, be absolutely sure that he's comfortable and does everything you ask at the walk, as well as the trot.

Move the Rib Cage

Moving the rib cage is the last part of body control. When you can control your horse's shoulders and hindquarters, his rib cage falls into place because he now understands moving away from leg pressure. Moving his ribs is simply a matter of positioning your feet.

Generally, you block your horse's forward motion with the bridle and use leg pressure in one of three spots on your horse's sides to control his body—toward the front to move his shoulders, in the middle to move his ribs, and toward the rear to move his hips. Pay attention to how your horse's rib cage feels under your leg. When you're aware of it, you begin to know when it's out of position and how to fix that.

- To move your horse's ribs, first gather and frame him, and block his forward motion with the reins. Put leg pressure right in the middle of his rib cage on first one side and then the other. He quickly figures out to move his ribs in either direction.

Use leg pressure toward the horse's front end to move his shoulders.

Leg pressure in the middle position moves the horse's ribs.

- When you bump your foot in the middle position, instead of your horse's rib cage bulging to the side under your leg, he should straighten through the middle and learn that his entire body can move sideways. Later you can use that tool to side-pass your horse or correct his position when he spins, for example.

- You might not realize how much a horse can drop his ribs to the outside during a circle, spin or rollback, or even when he backs. When his ribs move out of position, your horse's momentum is gone. He must learn that you can bump his rib cage back into position to straighten him and it's no big deal. When you control

his rib cage, your horse doesn't lose momentum, so his maneuvers are fluid and fast.

- One of the most important times to control your horse's ribs is when you move his front end to go into a spin, as he takes that initial step to cross his front legs. Many people but don't feel a horse's ribs fall out of position, but with his rib cage bowed to the outside, a horse can't spin fast and usually starts pivoting on the outside hind or both hind feet. He never sets his back end to spin because his rib cage position doesn't let him. When a horse's ribs are in line, he should be fairly straight in his turnarounds even though his head and neck might be curved a little into the spins.

- When you spin or roll your horse back in the direction you know isn't his naturally good side, pay attention to his rib cage when you start the turn. You might have to really straighten him through his body so he can move his front end freely in that direction. Gaining control of his rib cage allows you to do that.

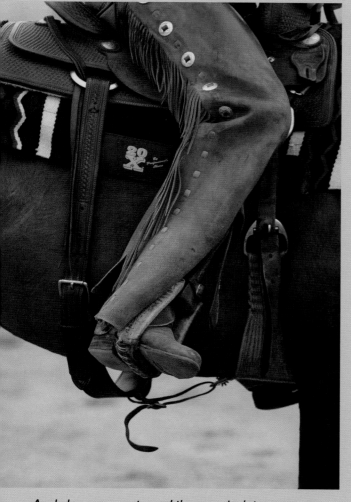

Apply leg pressure toward the rear cinch to move a horse's hips.

The better your horse understands ranch-riding basics, the better his foundation for advanced maneuvers.

8

GAITS, TRANSITIONS AND RANCH RIDING

Versatility ranch riding shows that a horse understands the basic gaits and making transitions from one gait to another, and that he can stop, turn and back. In addition to the walk, trot and lope, ranch riding also calls for a horse to travel in an extended trot and extended canter.

It might seem like the versatility ranch riding is just another western pleasure class, but it's not. American Quarter Horse Association rules, for example, describe the versatility horse moving at "working" or natural speed in the different gaits, and credit is given to the horse traveling with his head in a normal position. The judge looks for an alert, yet manageable horse, one that can hand gallop to a marker, stop, turn and jog off like it's no big deal.

Because a ranch-riding competitor must make changes at specific places, the horse and rider score well when each transition is on target. Transitions carry a lot of weight with a judge. Every transition should be as smooth as possible, and between the transitions a horse's gait should be consistent.

Some people might think they don't really need to prepare for the ranch riding class. That's not true. The better you and your horse perform the basic gaits and maneuvers, the better your score. And you also are better prepared for other parts of versatility competition because your horse is so light and responsive.

The Performance Goal

In ranch riding, you want your horse to travel smoothly in any gait, and you want to be confident that he can hold it steady, no matter the distance you travel. No matter the gait, his head carriage is

In versatility ranch riding the horse moves at steady, natural, working speed with natural head carriage.

natural, he's soft in the poll, and his body stays in a good frame. No matter if a transition is required in his gait, speed or direction, your horse is balanced and ready to make the change, and he's responsive so the changes come smoothly and easily.

These performance goals in versatility ranch riding probably are the same goals you had when you bought your first horse. No matter what you planned to do with your horse, you knew those three gaits and simple maneuvers were the basics, the starting point that would make your other riding plans happen. The basics still are the starting point for anything you do horseback.

If you do nothing but the basics, you can enjoy riding for years. When you do the basics in a way to develop your horse's lightness and control, you lay the foundation for so much more—reining, cutting and roping, whatever you want.

Review Your Skills

When you warm up your horse, get the fresh off first. Then ride him through the flexing, framing and body control exercises from the previous two chapters, or refer to the list in the back of the book. If your horse's response isn't as light as you'd like, work right there until it's soft before moving on to the next warm-up maneuver.

The Walk

My horse's walk in ranch riding isn't the typical gait seen in a western pleasure class. In the versatility class, my horse walks actively at a nice speed with his head nodding in a natural position.

To develop that walk, I build on skills my horse already has. He already knows how to flex at the poll and frame his body. Now he only needs to do those things often enough that he's comfortable and consistent gathering himself in an active, steady walk. When he's collected, he's ready to do anything, whatever I need.

You can develop that steady walk with your horse and without staying in the arena to do it. In fact, it's best if you work outside the arena in the open.

- Walk your horse across the pasture or down a trail, where he's relaxed, moves out freely and looks ahead. As he walks, pick up lightly on the reins and squeeze with your legs so that he softens his poll, rounds his back and frames his body.

- When you first gather and collect your horse while he walks, he probably can't hold that rounded frame very long. That's okay. It takes time for him to understand what you want and to build the muscle memory and stamina to hold that pretty frame.

- When you ask your horse for his head, he should give his nose to the pressure from your hands. If he doesn't, don't jerk the reins or fight him; just hold him. Lift your hands while you squeeze the horse forward with your legs. Hold your hands in position until he softens his poll, drops his nose and rounds his back. Then he's not traveling heavy on his forehand and strung out with his back flat.

- If necessary to frame your horse, bump his sides with the calves of your legs to drive his back end, so he really uses his hind legs to push forward.

- Any time you feel your horse push against the bit or flatten his back, lift your reins again to soften his poll and use your legs to gather his hindquarters underneath him. Then he's back in a collected position.

- The only way you can get comfortable keeping your horse in a good, soft frame is to ride him. Before long, he figures out what you want, and your hand and leg cues can become really subtle and soft.

- When you lift and squeeze to soften and frame your horse, he soon learns to prepare for a change, a maneuver. When he isn't prepared and in a balanced position, he can't perform well; his back is too flat for him to make a pretty turn or a soft stop. If you turn or stop a horse without gathering him and giving him an idea that change is coming, he usually throws his head, drops his shoulder, disengages his hip, and/or flattens his back, none desirable responses.

- Once your horse understands what you want when you lift your reins and squeeze

Even though a ranch-riding walk is an active, natural gait, the judge looks for a horse traveling in frame.

his sides, you have the foundation to do almost any maneuver. Plus, the maneuver seems soft and easy because your horse is in position to perform. His weight is balanced where it should be.

The Trot

In the trot, I also want my horse framed with good position to use his body effectively when we make a transition of some kind. He feels soft in my hands, drops his nose and flexes his poll. His back is softly rounded because he uses his hindquarters to propel himself forward in the trot.

For versatility ranch riding, I prefer a slow-to-medium trot and for my horse's head carriage to be natural. The trot is a steady, two-beat gait. It has cadence, what the judge looks for in ranch riding. An excessively slow or uncadenced trot should be penalized.

You can develop your horse's smooth, collected trot the same way you work on his walk. The only difference is he moves forward a little faster. Again, do this trotting work across your pasture, down a trail or in your arena.

A versatility horse should hold a cadenced, slow-to-medium jog while flexing easily at the poll and staying collected throughout the body.

- When you ask your horse to trot, slightly lift your reins and drive him forward with your legs, just like you do in the walk, but this time, smooch or kiss to him to go faster.

- Make a smooth transition. Don't spur your horse forward into a trot. You don't want him to think he has to hurry into the next gait when you lift your reins.

- As you trot, again, you want your horse soft at the poll with a round back—no head-throwing or cranking his tail. He should hold that nice frame and go faster. Looking at him from the side, his body position shouldn't change appreciably as he moves from a walk to the trot.

- If your horse really pushes into the bridle and trots inconsistently, don't hang onto his face with the reins or jerk them. Go back to the flexing and suppling exercises in your warm-up until he's soft in hand, or use the pull-to-the-hip exercise to lighten his response.

- If your horse has a naturally rough trot, you must really soften your lower back to accommodate the roughness, so it isn't so apparent to a judge. Remain upright, but soften your back from your waist down, so everything appears smooth in your upper body. That's showmanship.

The Extended Trot

Ranch versatility rules say it's okay to ride an extended trot while sitting or posting. I prefer the sitting trot. Some people prefer to post even though they also know judges might score them higher for sitting the trot, but that's their choice.

One rulebook calls the extended trot "an evident lengthening of stride from the regular trot with the same cadence, which causes an increase in speed." The obvious difference in speed comes from the horse striding out, increasing the length of his stride, not from moving his feet faster.

Some versatility competitors don't really show that distinct difference in speed from the jog to the extended trot. But because they think it looks faster, they sit a little more forward in their saddles or post. A judge can tell the difference. He knows when a horse really extends his trot and when the rider is trying to make it seem like the horse trots fast.

In the extended trot, the horse's feet don't move faster. Instead, the stride lengthens while the horse maintains cadence and a soft frame.

- To extend your horse's trot, do the same things you've been doing in the walk and jog. Lift your reins while you drive your horse's back end underneath his body to keep him in frame. You must really drive your horse with your seat. When you extend the trot, sit deeper in your saddle and drive your horse forward with your seat helping to push him.

- The harder your horse uses his hindquarters to drive himself forward, the deeper his hind legs reach under his body and the longer his stride becomes. Then he covers more ground more quickly than he does in the jog. That's a true extended trot when your horse lengthens his stride, stays in frame and works off his back end.

- At first, you might have to bump your horse's sides with your legs for him to figure out that it's okay to extend his trot and that he can do it without losing his collection, or frame. However, he might flatten out just a little in the extended trot. Give him time to understand.

- When your horse trots at any speed, you should hear a strong two-beat count from his front and back legs working together on the diagonal. His right front and left rear move together, and vice versa, to create that definite beat. Listen for that even cadence. That means your horse's legs are working as they should, with his body balanced as he moves.

The Lope

Your horse's lope should have a definite three-beat cadence. The cadence and speed in the lope might be different from that of the trot, but not your horse's softness and lightness. When you drive him forward into a lope, his poll should stay soft and his back rounded. Since he already knows how to move his hip, taking the correct lead shouldn't be a big deal.

The lope is where the time you spend working on your horse's body position and lightness pays off. You set him up to make a smooth transition into a lope on the correct lead. You have built a solid foundation for him to make that smooth canter departure.

- Be sure that you first ask for a soft frame before you cue your horse for the lead; otherwise, he might miss it. That frame tells him to prepare for a change. He's not caught off-guard, but instead probably gives you just a bit of extra attention.

- When your horse is framed and soft, direct him into whichever lead you want by using outside leg pressure. For a left lead, put pressure on his right side to push his hindquarters over and into the left lead. Do the reverse for a right lead, using your left leg to cue your horse. As you use leg pressure, smooch or kiss so your horse knows to move faster.

- The only way to help your horse figure out what you want is by being consistent. Smooching or kissing doesn't mean anything to your horse unless you routinely give the same cue and consistently ask for the same response. Your horse needs to understand only one thing: When he hears a smooch or kiss, he picks up the pace.

- You might have to really bump a young, green horse's side with your leg to get him to lope. At this point, he might not understand that the smooch or kiss means to move fast. So smooch first, before you use your legs, and give him an opportunity to do what you want before you use your leg. Before long, a colt figures out if he doesn't move when you smooch, your legs bump his sides, and he understands what you want.

- If you ask for that soft frame and cue your horse for a lope and he doesn't get it, don't grind on him all afternoon. Go back to the long-trot, jog and walk and be sure he stays soft in each of those gaits. When his body responds like you want, try loping again. Some young horses have a hard time going from an extended trot to a lope, but the horse can learn with time.

- If your horse doesn't transition smoothly from a walk to a trot, or to an extended trot, don't expect a smooth transition into a right or left lead. That's not to say that you don't lope your horse. But

When a horse understands lightness and body control, a canter departure is smooth, and the lope is soft and easy to ride.

the more time you spend teaching him soft transitions in a walk and trot, the more you can expect him to be light and gathered when you ask for a lope.

• Remember: A judge doesn't look at how hard you work to accomplish something with your horse. A judge looks for how smoothly and efficiently you get the job done when you ask your horse to lope in the correct lead.

The Extended Lope

Ranch versatility guidelines for riding the extended lope are similar to those for extending the trot. The cadence remains the same, and an obvious lengthening of that horse's stride causes an increase in controlled speed. The change in gait to an extended lope should be a smooth transition, and a judge wants to see that obvious difference in speed, in other words, he wants to see that longer stride.

As with the extended trot, an extended lope demonstrates controlled speed due to a lengthening of the horse's stride.

- The only way to make any transition smooth is to be sure that your horse's poll and back are soft. Then he's balanced to go faster or slower without the change being a big deal.

- Lope your horse in a soft frame, and then lift and hold his face slightly as you ask him to extend his lope. Use your outside leg against your horse's side so that he understands to lope in the correct lead, smooch and lean slightly forward so your horse knows it's okay to go faster.

- Faster doesn't mean uncontrolled. Faster means your horse's stride lengthens as he extends his lope, and he covers more ground faster than he does at a slow lope. The flexing and body-control exercises give you the tools to extend his stride.

- Gradually increase your horse's speed until it's what you want, and then ask him to hold steady at that speed.

- Your horse shouldn't hit a run immediately; then you have to rate him back to a hand gallop. He might go too slowly, so then you might have to pick up your horse's speed again. That's not what a judge wants to see.

- If your horse doesn't hold a steady pace at the extended lope, work with him at home until he does. Usually, if you've gone through that progression, asking him to soften at the poll and through the back, and to hold a steady gait when he walks, jogs, long-trots or lopes, your horse shouldn't be difficult to rate when he extends his lope.

- Remember that your horse already understands the rate cues at the slower gaits; you need only to make them consistently a few times at the extended lope. Then your horse realizes that everything still applies, and the only thing different, once again, is the speed of his gait.

- One caution: A horse that's loping sometimes goes off-lead in the back end when you ask him to pick up the pace. Consciously hold your outside leg on your horse when you smooch and ask for that transition and speed. No matter how confident you are that your horse can stay on lead, your leg is insurance that he stays correct.

Transitions

The ranch-riding pattern in the versatility class has both upward and downward transitions, and a judge docks you points for breaking gait. You also lope, stop, and then trot out of the rollback. That's tough to do since everyone usually lopes out of rollbacks in the reining. Trotting out of the rollback is a real test of skill in transitions and can be one of the little things that help a judge make his choice in ranch riding.

- When you do the work at home, you have smooth transitions at the show. They result from riding your horse. That's how your horse learns your cues.

- If you've been riding and doing the things discussed so far, your horse basically comes to you when you lift the reins. You can move his shoulders and his hips, and he's not frightened or aggressive. You have the control you need physically for smooth transitions.

- The main thing about a smooth transition: You also must manage the mental aspect of making that change. Have in mind exactly what you want your horse to do.

- Practice making transitions with your horse at home. Pick a spot across the pen or pasture and plan to change gait or direction there. Think about making that smooth, easy transition, then ride your horse through the change.

The Stop

Although there is more information about rundowns and stops in a later chapter, the only way I can have a soft, smooth stop with a horse is to position his body to make one. I lay the groundwork now for a pretty stop later by teaching my horse to be soft when I pick up on the reins and to gather himself when I use my legs.

To my horses, the word "whoa" means stop—nothing else. The only time I say whoa is when I want my horse at a standstill. The lift of my reins tells him something different is coming. Whoa is even more precise; it tells him a stop is next.

- The best thing you can do to make stops easy on your horse is to be consistent. When your stop cues are consistent, your horse can figure out what you want.

- The way you say whoa tells your horse more about the stop that is coming. If you want a soft, smooth, easy-into-the-ground stop, say "whoooaaa" slowly and softly.

- Yelling whoa is like having a light turn red in front of your truck. You slam on the brakes and stop, but it's not soft, smooth or pretty. People who yell whoa also seem to have fast hands and pull the reins faster and harder than necessary.

- Before you work on your horse's stop, first be sure he really understands how to flex at his poll and round his back. He must be soft in hand when traveling in any gait.

- To stop your horse, lift the reins to ask for softness at the poll and say whoa, using your legs lightly to gather his back end underneath him.

- If your horse doesn't stop promptly, but dribbles down to a walk and then stops, use your feet to really drive his back end underneath him. As you collect his back end, don't jerk on the reins. Instead, after you lift them, use your reins as a block. Hold your horse's face in that elevated position as you drive his hindquarters forward. The bit becomes a wall you drive him toward until he softens his spine and stops to keep from hitting the wall. When it's his choice, your horse figures out how not to hit that wall.

- If your horse's stop is not smooth and collected, try to figure out what the problem is. Does he push against your hands when you lift the reins, or does his back stay flat and hollow? Maybe he doesn't really grasp yet what you want him to do. You might need more lift in the reins or to bump him more with your legs, so that his weight is better distributed to make the stop.

- When your horse's weight is on the forehand, his stop is rough because his spine is flat, rather than soft and slightly arced underneath you. Go back to work on those basics. Be sure your horse responds to pressure from your hands and legs. Walk and stop your horse several until he responds, as he should. Then trot and stop him.

- If you've taught your horse to respond properly to your hands and legs, he can figure out how to stop smoothly, as long as you aren't too fast with your hands. When you pull too fast or too hard on his face, a horse gets cranky when he hears whoa. He anticipates the jerk and stops hard with stiff front legs because he's trying to protect his mouth. When a horse pushes on the bit, he also stops on his front feet. Be light with your hands and give your horse time for his stop to become soft.

In ranch riding competition, a horse must stop on target, right at the cone, as described in the pattern.

- When your horse stops smoothly at the walk, trot and stop him. If he responds well and stays soft, he understands how to position his body, and you can progress through the gaits. Work to maintain smoothness and collection in the stop from any gait or speed.

The Back

The key to smoothness in all the gaits and the stop is teaching your horse to flex at the poll every time you pick up the reins and to drive with his hindquarters to round his spine. The same is true with when you back your horse. Again, there is more information about using the back with your stop in a later chapter, but you must lay the foundation now for those advanced maneuvers.

- When you ask your horse to back, pick up and hold the reins like you have in previous sessions, then drive your horse into the maneuver with your legs. The difference is that you don't back that horse off your hands so much as off your feet and body motion. When you block forward motion and don't pull on your horse's face, he figures out to go back. The minute he takes a step back, release him so he understands what you want.

- You might have to wait awhile for your horse to take that first step back. Be very patient and keep blocking his forward motion. Don't pull, but don't give either; just hold. Be sure to release him immediately when he steps back.

- Initially, your horse might be resistant and have a hard time backing. Don't just pull, pull, pull on the reins; that's the wrong thing to do. Hold him with your reins and give him time to figure out what you want. Start slow. He can't back fast or far at first.

- If you've done the previous body control exercises and taught your horse to move his hips, a crooked back is no problem. If your horse's hip moves off that straight line, put your leg along his side to move his hip where you want it. With a colt you usually don't have quite that much backend control, but you will after he's

Flexion and softness are just as important when backing a horse as they are when traveling with forward motion.

progressed to the lightness and control exercises. On a colt, don't worry if his back isn't straight.

- If your horse understands backing, but becomes sluggish, reinforce that you want him to back faster by bumping—not spurring—with both legs. Use the calves of your leg and the inside of your feet to bump his sides. Using a spur at this stage only makes a horse nervous, and if he anticipates the spur, he can become resentful and cranky.

- Be careful with a really resistant horse that simply refuses to back. He could come over backward with you. That's dangerous. Get some professional help whenever a horse really locks up and backing becomes a real problem. Also check your horse's back and stifle joints for soreness, which also can cause a horse to be resistant.

The Reverse

The next chapter has more about advanced maneuvers—the side-pass, rollback and spin. For now, teach your horse to make a simple reverse and how to reverse in a walk or trot. At a show the reverse you make depends on what the judge wants.

- If the judge wants you to reverse your horse in forward motion, at a walk or trot, for example, your horse should be gathered and soft in that gait. Don't stop and make a pivot-type turn; calmly walk or trot your horse in a round, little circle and go the other way.

- For a simple reverse, stop your horse. Pick up the reins slightly because you want him to be soft and in frame. Then ask your horse to walk his front end around in a 180-degree turn until he's headed in the other direction. Use leg pressure to keep his rib cage in position as you turn.

- A reverse doesn't have to be fast. Shoot for a smooth turn with your horse crossing his front legs and having a good rhythm, or cadence, as he crosses them.

- If the show pattern requires you to reverse at a cone, stop with your horse's hip right at the cone. Do the perfect pivot, and his hip should still be at the cone for the next maneuver.

Ranch Riding Showmanship

The versatility ranch riding might be held as a completely separate class, or you might complete the trail course and then move immediately to the rail for ranch riding. Here are some things to keep in mind when you show in ranch-riding competition.

- No. 1: Know the ranch-riding pattern you're expected to follow. The rules might suggest a pattern, but a judge usually can change the pattern as long as all the required maneuvers are included. His instructions might be posted with the pattern before the competition, and if you're lucky, you might be able to ask him questions about the pattern, but that isn't always possible.

- Before you start riding through your pattern, acknowledge the judge with a nod, if possible. Then he knows that you're ready to perform.

When a pattern requires a side-pass, your leg should be right at the cone.

If you must stop, turn and lope away from a cone, put your horse's hip at the cone so you can turn and stay lined up with the cone.

When the pattern includes a stop or turn on the forehand, your horse's shoulder should be at the cone.

Make any transitions in the ranch-riding pattern right on target with the markers.

- Make your transitions in the arena right on target with the cones, or markers.

- If the pattern requires that you side-pass, for example, your leg should be right at the cone when you stop. If you must stop, turn and lope away from the cone, put your horse's hip at the cone so you can turn and stay lined up with it. If the pattern requires a turn on the forehand, your horse's shoulder should be at the cone. Also stop with your horse's shoulder on the cone when you back to the next cone; otherwise, the judge won't think you've backed far enough for a good score.

- Don't overprepare your horse before the ranch riding, stopping or spinning him repeatedly. He can become aggravated and sore. Ride to keep him fit and maybe do a few downward transitions to be sure he's light in hand, but don't overschool your horse on maneuvers.

- The closer to competition time, the more pressure people seem to put on their horses. That can really blow your performance. Back off even though that can be mentally hard to do. Don't leave your best rides in the practice pen.

- You can't teach your horse much during a show, so don't step up your training program in the warm-up pen. Keep it the same, and don't ask more of your horse than he knows to do. Then, when you go back home, continue your training, and you will wind up with a really nice horse. But if you hammer on him at the show, he starts dreading any event and all the maneuvers he must perform.

9

THE SIDE-PASS, ROLLBACK AND SPIN

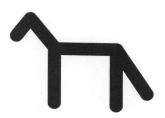

Working on a side-pass or spin is a lot like teaching a horse to back; it's one step at a time. It might seem like it takes months, but when you get that first step, it's great. Now that you've taken the time to develop body control and lightness, you'll be surprised by what your horse can do when you apply the right kind of pressure at the right time.

The important thing with any new manuever: Show your horse what you want and give him time to figure out things instead of making him do the maneuver. Time keeps him from developing anxiety about being forced to do something he doesn't understand. Give your horse time to understand.

Even though I take my time on these maneuvers with my horses, I often work a horse on turnarounds, rollbacks and side-passes during the same ride. My horse can be at different stages in each maneuver, so

I'm careful to work in increments so my horse stays relaxed and comfortable with whatever we do.

The Performance Goal

Riding your horse through a nice side-pass, rollback or spin is part of the payoff when you take the time to develop body control and a soft, responsive horse. Ideally, before working on these advanced maneuvers, you can cue your horse to move different parts of his body and have taught him to be collected and light. For the side-pass, rollback and spin, you combine the things he knows in different ways and then take those skills into the versatility trail course, ranch riding, cutting and working ranch-horse classes.

Advanced maneuvers aren't only for the show arena. You side-pass to open a gate at home or

When a horse is given enough time to understand the spin and how to do it, he can build speed and remain comfortable and relaxed.

roll your horse over his hocks to head a cow and send it back to the herd. Anything new that you and your horse can accomplish only makes you better partners—even the spin. It might not have as much practical use, for example, as other maneuvers, but when you can turn your horse around smoothly and easily, the two of you are really communicating.

Review Your Skills

As usual, check your horse's response with the flexing and suppling exercises discussed in the previous chapters. Remember to improve any response that isn't as light as you think it should be before moving on to other maneuvers. A complete list of these suppling exercises follows the last chapter.

The Side-Pass

There's no reason you can't side-pass your horse if you've taught him to flex his head, move his shoulders and hips, and gather himself when you pick up the reins. You already should be able to move a front foot a step or two and drop your foot back to move the hind feet, too. Side-passing your horse is a matter of combining these simple things and showing your horse that's what you want him to do.

- To side-pass your horse, pick up both reins slightly to block his forward motion and put a "wall" in front of him. The bump him in the rib cage with your right foot and leg to move his body left, or vice versa. Don't kick or spur; just bump with your outside foot.

When teaching the side-pass, sometimes using a fence as a barrier to forward motion helps a horse figure out the desired response.

- Give your horse time to figure out what you want. It's claustrophobic to a horse's mind when you block his forward motion with the reins and push him with a foot. He feels trapped and doesn't know what to do. Go slowly and give him time to take that first step. Then he learns where that "out" is, away from your foot, and he relaxes and understands what you want.

- It can help to use a fence as a barrier when teaching the side-pass. Position your horse with his head toward the fence. Don't turn his face right or left, but use both reins and the fence to block his forward motion. Then bump your horse's rib cage with your lower leg to direct him to the side. With the fence there, if your horse wants to go forward, you don't have to pull much with the bridle. You only lift the reins to keep your horse gathered and rounded, so his back isn't flat when you ask him to move off your leg.

- At first, to help your horse understand, you might allow his forehand and hindquarters to move separately as he tracks to the side. Keep him gathered and put up the wall with your reins. Try to move his rib cage first. If he moves his front end more than the back end, drop your foot back to step the hips over a bit. Adjust your foot to help keep his shoulder, ribs and hips in line. Don't be aggressive at all; you just want the horse to understand what you're asking of him. Give him time to understand.

- Any horse, especially a young horse, might have trouble moving his feet to the side; that must feel weird to him. When he takes that step or two, stop, rub him and sit still a bit. When he feels comfortable after taking that first step, he might take two or three more. Work on the side-pass slowly—even when you really must focus to get that first step and even if that step has a little forward motion.

- Most people ask for only a step or two when they first side-pass a horse, and that's fine. But when you really have built control of the front end and hindquarters and can gather your horse, you might push him to the side, and he could side-pass 7 feet. That's because

you've done everything ahead of time; the parts are all in place.

- When you side-pass to the left, at first you might tip your horse's nose a little to the point you can see his right eye. That helps make it easy for him to go sideways, but a horse usually straightens as he progresses. In the end, you want him to tip his nose in the same direction you want him to go.

- If your horse locks up a little while he's learning, give him a minute or two to get his mind back into his feet. In other words, feel your horse. If he's tight and tense, relax; you've put too much pressure on him too quickly. Back off until he understands that he can't go forward, but can go sideways off your leg. Let him figure out that.

- As your horse progresses, side-pass him 8 or 9 feet one way, then let him walk down the fence. Circle him back around to it and then side-pass him down the fence in the other direction.

- As soon as your horse understands and side-passes freely each way on the fence, try side-passing him in the open. Most people should be able to do that within about three days, but that depends on the horse. That's sure not the case for a colt with only 30 days' riding.

- Teach the side-pass slowly. If you can move your horse one way and then the other, quit for the day. Come back to the side-pass the next day. If your horse takes a few more steps, feels soft in hand, and seems to understand what you want, you probably can ask him to leg-yield out in the open on the third day.

The 12-Foot Box

Here's something my wife, Holly, showed me, and it's a good all-around body-control exercise. I use it to keep my horse responsive when he moves his shoulders and hips, and side-passes.

- Make a 12-foot box in your arena. Draw a box in the dirt or use four posts to make the box.

121

- Put your horse's head and front legs inside the box with his hind legs on the other side of a post or line. Side-pass him right or left to the next corner of the square. Then move your horse's hindquarters around the corner, so that he's in position to side-pass down the next side of the box, with his forehand still inside and his hind legs outside the box. Be sure to work your horse in both directions.

- Now put your horse's hindquarters inside the 12-foot box with his head and forelegs outside the box. Side-pass him down one side of the box. Now move your horse's shoulders and bring his forehand around the corner on the outside, so he's in position to side-pass down the next side of the box. Again, be sure to work your horse in both directions.

- Any time your horse becomes a little anxious or aggravated, quit. Let him stand there and mellow out. When he's calm, instead of continuing to work around the box, you might go to the fence to side-pass him. Any time your horse gets tense, back off and go slow with him. Let him walk in some 15-foot circles. If he feels pressured, nobody can teach him anything.

Add to Your Skills: The Rollback

The AQHA versatility ranch-riding pattern transitions normally include a lope, stop and a rollback with the horse trotting out of the rollback. That's tough because most people are used to loping out of a rollback in the dry work for the ranch-horse class. A versatility rider really must have control of his horse for the rollbacks in competition.

A judge can knock off 2 points for breaking gait if a horse lopes when he should trot out of the ranch-riding rollback. When a horse is pumped to compete, gearing him down to trot out of the rollback is a real test of skill. Then later, when he should lope from the rollbacks in the ranch-horse pattern, the judge can score him down for trotting.

Too, there's a difference between the reiner-type rollback and the type move a cutter uses. I prefer the cutter-style rollback because my horses must work cattle whether they're at a show or not. For me, that style rollback is a more versatile maneuver, and it seems easy for my horse, too.

Obviously my horse must really listen to me to know whether to trot or lope out of a rollback. When he does the right thing, it's only because we've done our work before the show. He knows my cues well, and that comes from riding my horse. That's how any horse learns—from the riding.

- The reiner-type rollback has forward motion. The horse runs and stops, and when he rolls back to the left, the left hind is his pivot foot. But he rolls only partway around, not the full 180, before he lopes in the correct, left lead. Instead of coming completely back through his hocks in the turn, he seems almost arced when he leaves the rollback. That's because he pivots and pushes off his left hind and can go only so far around the turn. If he turns the complete 180, he can't push off that left leg.

- In the cutting world, when a horse is started on a cow and the cow turns, the horse backs into the turn and then moves across the pen with the cow. Backing through the turn helps a cutting horse to learn how to get into and out of the turn effectively. When a horse backs into a left rollback, for example, he uses his offside, right leg to push. That's how he leads with the left leg to make a smooth departure out of a rollback. He can't do that pushing off the left pivot leg.

- To teach the cutter-type rollback, circle your horse in a walk to the left. With his face arced to the left, stop and back him. As you back, use your left leg to move your horse's hip to the outside, the right, and back him in a right-hand circle, keeping his face to the left. Do the opposite to back your horse the other direction. Go slowly. Most horses, even mature ones, never have been asked to back like this.

- While backing to the right, your horse's rib cage is slightly out of alignment, which allows his front legs to cross over to the left. Then you must bring his nose and push his leading left shoulder through the turn, and his rib cage must follow the shoulder's lead.

A horse backs into a cutter-style rollback...

... and then makes the turn.

- As you back your horse in a circle and ask him to roll back cutter-style to the left, his left hind moves back, so your horse easily can bring his body around to the left. As he pivots left, he pushes off on his outside right hind and moves smoothly into the left lead.

- When you first back your horse in a circle, let him come out of it in a walk. Walk a few minutes, then set him up again to back in the circle. Do that five or six times, letting your horse walk out of it, and your horse figures out the rollback. He starts moving his front end freely and really loads his right hind because he wants to get out of the backing. Backing is hard. Again, work your horse in each direction.

- At home, bring your horse through the rollback turn with one hand or two. Either way, you want your horse to look in the direction he's rolling back, so pick up the inside shoulder and let him come through the turn as smoothly as he can.

- Don't put much pressure on your horse at the beginning when he's learning about rollbacks. When you use too much pressure, a horse gets bracey and stiff. Take it slow and soon your horse doesn't mind stopping and turning at all.

- When you leave a rollback, teach your horse that pressure from both legs means to trot, but pressure from only one leg (the outside leg) means to lope. Keep your horse collected, and then use the correct leg pressure to leave the rollback in the required gait.

- When you put both legs on your horse and trot out of the rollback consistently at home, your horse learns to hold the trot. Then he can do that in the ranch riding competition.

- When you want to lope out of a rollback in the left lead at home, use only your right leg on your horse and cluck or smooch to him. Use your left leg when you want a right lead. That cluck or a smooch means for him to go faster, and pressure from one leg is his cue to lope. Do that consistently at home, and you also can do that in the ranch-horse patterns.

- When a horse doesn't quite know how to lope out of the rollback, work with him at home. Back him into those circles and let him learn to move his front end slowly at first. Then pick up speed and hit a lope. He might jog a couple of strides, but too much pressure here can scare him. However, don't let your horse trot out of rollbacks very long because you don't want him to make a habit of doing that.

- If your horse continues to trot and doesn't lope on cue, then you must put on the pressure. Stop, roll him back and drive him right out of the turn. You also might stop and back your horse into the turn, but instead of a 180, do a complete 360 revolution, and then drive him out of the turn at a lope.

- When it's really hard to drive your horse into the lope, squeeze his rib cage and smooch. If he doesn't lope, slap down his outside hind leg with the rein. You might have to do that only once. The next time you squeeze and smooch, the horse usually lopes. Using the rein sometimes is more effective than using a spur because the rein on the leg really drives a horse's back end underneath him.

- A common rollback problem: Going into the stop, you have too much slack in your reins. When you realize that, your hands get fast, and you jerk your horse into the maneuver. Instead, collect your horse before the stop, lifting the reins slightly and driving his back end. Then quietly ask for the stop.

- Another common problem occurs if you turn your horse before the stop is complete. Then the horse is out of balance and can miss the lead. Instead, when you stop for the rollback, mentally count, "One, two." Then ask for the rollback. Stop your horse completely. If he feels you wanting to roll him back too quickly, he braces in the stop, and it's not straight or soft.

- Loping out of a rollback doesn't mean your horse runs wide open. You want him gathered and coming to your bridle, not flattening his back or pushing against your hand. Then you can perform whatever maneuver comes next. If your horse gets really pushy leaving the rollback, flex him down right then and pull him to your hip. (See Chapter 6.)

- Showmanship in the rollback is all about smoothness, from the stop to coming out of the turn on the correct lead.

- If you do leave a rollback in the wrong lead, a judge doesn't get you for that until you start into a circle on the incorrect lead. You definitely must change to the correct lead before starting the circle.

The Spin

When it comes to spins, most people worry about locking down a horse's back end. They don't think about moving the front end.

That's the goal—move the front end. Once that basic concept is in mind, a rider can really make some progress.

A spin isn't so much a horse holding a pivot foot or a rider moving his hand right or left. A spin results when the rider can lighten his horse's front end and move his front feet. When a horse is really riding and listening, and the rider moves his hand, the horse's shoulder automatically comes right underneath that hand. The rider doesn't have to pull his horse's face. The front end moves around the turn with his hand, and when it does, the back end finally stops.

A spin is simple when you get in your mind exactly what you want your horse to do. You pick up the reins, but don't have to move your hand much. Your horse basically comes to you. He's not frightened or aggressive, and he turns around without a worry. If you've

Walking a horse in small circles helps him figure out how to cross one front leg over the other and eventually move his front end around his hindquarters.

never ridden spins when you don't have to pull on the horse, it's hard to realize that you can move your hand slightly here or there and the horse can do phenomenal things.

Nice spins come from building softness, body control and smooth transitions. Your horse really rides between your bridle reins and your legs. There's so much more to that comment than people realize.

- Think about the concept of a spin. Your horse's front end moves around his hindquarters. Concentrate on moving your horse's forehand.

- In the spin, most people try to hold a horse's back end and stick him with the outside foot. The horse automatically gets stiff and rigid. His face wants to come back to the foot that kicks him, so his face wants to go in the wrong direction. Now the horse is scared and doesn't want to come around softly at all when he turns.

- Show your horse how to move his front end. Start walking him in circles twice his body length, and get him busy at it. Then gradually close the circles down to a horse length, 6 or 7 feet. When your horse really walks in a lot of small circles, he learns how to move his front end fluidly. Once he does, you can stop his back end with an indirect rein.

- Teach your horse to walk the circles as fast as he can, and he must cross his front legs. He might not cross them completely at first, but as the circles get small his front legs must cross. Your horse doesn't know how to do that fast until you help him build the muscle memory. You always want your horse's nose coming to the inside of your circle at a 45-degree angle at first. Keep in mind that his nose is connected to his inside front foot, and make sure his neck stays soft.

- That fast, steady walk develops the cadence your horse later has in his spins. To increase his speed and the cadence, bump with your outside foot and gradually tighten that circle. Your horse soon figures out that it's easier to hold his back end in place and walk around it.

- After walking your horse in a few small circles, walk away from the circle a distance before you bring him back into another circle. Make sure that you always bring his nose around first, that his nose and his inside front foot are going in the same direction, and that his neck is soft.

- Moving in and out of circles at a walk or jog teaches your horse how to go quietly into and out of any maneuver and make those transitions. Some horses spin well, but have a hard time starting the maneuver, and this exercise can make that an easy transition.

- Walking circles also gives your horse time to understand what you want and helps you develop your timing. You must know when to put pressure on your horse for a spin. That's timing and feel. In the circles, as you learn to move into the spin, you feel when that crossover is correct, and your horse does, too. Everything is quiet and smooth. But you sure-enough must understand that timing and smoothness before you pressure your horse to come through the turns fast. That's where walking circles pays off.

- When your horse is comfortable walking tight circles, pick up the reins slightly and try to move his outside shoulder across to the inside as you bump his rib cage with your outside leg. Keep his nose at a 45-degree angle to the inside and make sure you release your inside leg pressure. If you've done the homework on moving the front end, your horse might take several crossover steps, but if he takes only a step or two, that's great. Then walk him in a circle.

- When he turns around, your horse's body should be a little arced into his turn, and his nose should be leading his front foot. Make sure he stays soft through his neck. You might tip a young horse into the turn a bit more, just so he learns he can do that. Otherwise, in time he can get stiff and put his head more to the outside.

- Sometimes when a horse moves his shoulders and feet, but not very fast, he

The best way to show a horse's spin is to set him up to start the maneuver correctly and add gain speed.

starts hopping or his feet get tangled. Trot him in a 10-foot circle, but keep bumping his nose at a 45-degree angle to the inside and keep him soft though his neck. Remember that you need to teach your horse to move his front feet. If your horse is stiff through the neck, he's stiff in his shoulders. With stiff shoulders your horse cannot move his front feet.

• When your horse is learning to walk down into a spin and cross his legs, don't worry about speed or momentum at this point because your horse doesn't really understand things. Speed comes later.

• While your horse learns, pay attention to his hip as you bring him down into the crossovers. His back end shouldn't move around much. His rib cage probably will be arced a little to the outside. For that

nice reiner-style spin, you must control your horse's rib cage and, more than anything, maintain collection. Without collection, there is no softness.

• After your horse learns to move his front end around his back end, smooch two or three times to help him understand that it's okay to keep going in the turn. Smooch more in the beginning and then try to refrain from smooching much so that later your horse associates the smooch with speed and connects that cue with your outside foot.

• What you're trying to achieve when you walk your horse into a spin is for him to stay in the spin without you having continually to turn him. So walk him into a spin. Lead his front inside foot by bumping his nose to the inside while you bump with your outside leg. Put your horse into the spin and then release him, and when he gets out of place, put the horse back into the spin and then release him again, and so on, so that he learns to stay in the correct position.

- How fast your horse progresses with spins depends on his age. For a 2-year-old being put under saddle, walking in circles is enough. A 2-year-old needs more time than an older horse to understand the maneuver, and the young horse's body isn't prepared for as much work. A 3-year-old's mind is becoming seasoned enough for the work if he's been ridden like he should, and his body is mature enough to handle learning more advanced maneuvers. A mature horse that's broke, but not really trained, should be able to walk around in a 360, crossing over correctly, within about a week—if you do things correctly. That's not to say the horse is fast, just correct. Within that week, the horse might walk his front end around really well in one direction, but not the other way.

- Don't drill and drill a horse, even a mature one. He gets tired and resentful. Keep the moves fresh. When he walks a 360 turnaround comfortably the first time, say whoa, let him stand and rub him. The next time, walk him out of the turn and into a circle. Keep changing what you do.

- Work on the body control and lightness exercises listed in the warm-up, so that you don't have to really kick your horse in the turnarounds. When you add speed to your spins and kick a lot, a horse gets cranky in his work.

- Instead of extreme kicking in the spin, take your horse across the pen and ask for a leg-yield—pretty hard. This can invigorate his turnaround work without him associating the extra pressure from the leg yield with the spin. Ask him to yield to your leg when you have forward motion. Smooch every time before the leg-yield so your horse associates your smooch with vigorous movement. Work on the leg-yield in both directions until your horse really responds and then

let him relax. Now go back to the spin, smooch to your horse and try to leave your foot alone so that he moves off the smooch, maybe one per revolution. That cue is the thing. Use your foot if his rib cage pops out of place.

Showmanship and Spins

Like so many people, when I first started showing my horses, I wanted to hurry through the maneuvers. Here are a few things I've learned about spins since then.

- Because often there is only one spin each direction in the versatility working ranch-horse pattern, most people try to make each spin really fast, and they usually overshoot the mark. The more your horse spins beyond the 360-degree turn, the more points you lose.

- The best approach for a spin is to set up your horse so he can be correct as he comes through the turn and then stop right on target. Give him a step or two to get organized. Otherwise, the spin falls apart. Let your horse get into the spin before you add speed. Then he's correct when you smooch for speed, and the spin looks good.

- Don't set up your horse to look bad. Push him faster than he can go, and his spins look terrible. Be smooth. If your horse isn't really fast, but is correct at a medium speed, you don't lose any points, and you might gain a half-point. The thing about showing: You must stay out of the penalty box.

- If it's difficult for your horse to start the spin from a dead stop, ride him forward a step into the spin. Some horses can spin from a standstill, but some need that one step to go smoothly into a spin.

- That first step forward also gives you a chance to move your horse's rib cage. If he's still setting back from a stop, on his first step into the spin his rib cage might poke out to the side. The horse might be able to do a rollback, but he can't make a pretty 360; his body is too bunched up. With that one step forward, he can be in position to turn.

- As you go into a left spin, for example, lead with your inside left leg, or vice versa, so that your leg isn't in your horse's way. That's part of a pretty transition into the turnaround.

- Sometimes a rider moves his head into the turn and brings his horse to his head, and so forth around the spin. That's jerky. Instead, look slightly ahead of your horse as he turns. The steadier your gaze, the steadier your horse can be.

- Sometimes a horse wants to pick up or shuffle his other leg—not the pivot foot—during a spin. As long as that other foot isn't moving in a 2-foot circle, a judge doesn't discredit you. But he can if your horse takes a big step with his back end. However, if your horse's rib cage is where it should be, he probably won't take that step.

- Your horse might have to use that outside pivot foot a little as he spins, but as he picks up speed, he usually switches back to the inside pivot foot. He's more balanced that way when you increase the speed correctly by pushing his rib cage, not just the shoulder. Push only the shoulder across, and his rib cage falls out of position. Then he stays on the outside hind foot and can't spin as fast.

- Never let your horse stop turning around until you say whoa. He must know to keep doing whatever you ask until you ask him to quit. Don't get into a habit of turning around one time and letting your

horse stop. Later, you might turn once and feel him hesitate, then spin again and hesitate again because you've let him stop after one turnaround. He should continue turning until you say whoa. Consistency with that is important.

The Barn Magnet

If you don't understand the ins and outs of riding a young horse, before long you both can be frustrated. Your colt doesn't have anything against you; a horse doesn't think that way, but he can learn how to cheat you a little bit, usually on the barn-side of the pen. Use that to advantage.

When any colt I ride thinks about the barn, it becomes a magnet pulling at him each time he's along the barn side of my pen. It's hard to turn a young horse away from any magnet, whether it's the barn or another horse in a pen nearby.

When I recognize that feel, I use that magnet to advantage to teach my colt about turning. Then my barn magnet becomes one of the best training tools I can have. I use what my colt wants—the security of the barn—to set him up for the turn I want. Then I don't get mad, and my colt doesn't get hot.

I set up my colt to turn toward the magnet. By teaching the first steps that way, my colt wants to take them and usually steps his front end around toward the magnet. I can build on those first steps to get more steps away from the magnet. Before long the colt figures out what I want and does a full turnaround.

That barn magnet is a little thing, but it works, and not only with colts, to draw a horse into a turn.

Smooth acceleration, a soft stop and easy backing begin with basic transitions.

10

THE RUNDOWN, STOP AND BACK

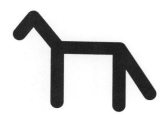

Most people can run a horse down the middle of a pen and get him stopped, but it's not always pretty. To score well in the ranch-horse class dry work, the reining pattern, a horse must accelerate smoothly as he runs and be soft in hand when he stops and backs the required distance.

That horse has what's called rate; he's in control. He doesn't push against the bit when the rider asks for a transition, but responds to his rider's cues. That horse is as easy to stop as he is to ask for speed.

Teaching your horse that ratability starts with those simple upward and downward transitions in the previous ranch-riding chapter. If your horse can't make those basic changes softly, he can't stop smoothly later. The foundation for a reining-type stop isn't there.

You have the foundation when you consistently can make a soft downward transition from a fast lope to a slow lope, for example, or from a lope to a jog. You can pick up your reins to make the transition, and your horse melts in your hand and underneath you without any resistance.

The Performance Goal

Yes, you go fast in the versatility reining work, but you aren't out of control. That control is the real test. Your horse extends his lope, but shuts it off when you ask him to stop. He's soft in his back when you say whoa and isn't resistant when you pick up the reins for any maneuver.

If you've been doing the warm-up exercises in previous chapters, you've been doing all the little things

Simple transitions develop ratability, the foundation for soft, smooth stops that build confidence in both the horse and rider.

that make up the big maneuvers you need for a good score in a reining pattern, especially those rundowns and stops. Trust in your preparation and step up to the next level.

Even if you never run a reining pattern, being able to go fast and know that you can stop your horse is one of the best confidence-builders. Knowing you have that control makes you feel like you can do anything with your horse.

Making that good stop with control also takes confidence. The best way to be confident enough to try for that big stop is to ride your horse and do your homework. Teach him what he needs to know to be soft and light, and ride him enough to know that he will be responsive.

You can lose confidence so much faster than you can regain it, but when you build your control a step at a time, you build your confidence, too.

Review Your Skills

Remember to loosen up your horse and get the fresh off him before you start working on any advanced maneuvers. Doing some of the basic flexion and suppling routines (listed at the end of the book) in your warm-up helps you get a feel for your horse's frame of mind that particular day.

"When you establish rate with your horse, you establish control."

When making an upward transition to an extended lope, a horse should extend the stride in a collected, controlled manner, not run wide open.

Establish Rate

When you establish rate with your horse, you establish control. Developing rate is the next step in preparing your horse for ranch versatility dry work. When he is soft through his spine and in your hands as he slows down and speeds up, he can learn to stop softly and stay in good frame.

- Don't try to work on rate when your horse is fresh. Even when you gyp him around the pen and he gets tired, he still can be pushy when you get on him. You must teach your horse to rate while you're on his back.

- If you don't think your horse responds as he should during the warm-up, keep working on the transitions and the suppling exercises until he responds. If he isn't responsive doing the basic things, he isn't ready to for you to ask more of him in any advanced maneuver.

- Try to figure out when your horse's mind is right for rating him and doing downward transitions. You can call that horsemanship, or you might call it feel or timing, but it's the difference between trainers and people who just ride. Learn to read your horse.

When making a downward transition, a horse shouldn't resist slowing, but remain in frame and responsive to the rider's cues.

The slower speed in a downward transition from an extended lope to a slow lope results when the horse's stride shortens.

- Your horse can learn about rate so much easier when he's not running wide open. Later, when he understands what you want, you can pick up the speed.

- In an extended trot, for example, your horse should drive his hind legs deep underneath his body yet be soft in the poll and responsive to your hands. As he rates to the jog, his body should hold that same frame and continue to be soft in hand.

- When you teach your horse rate, quietly pick up on the reins and slow him to the speed you want. When he slows, immediately give slack in the reins. If you don't, your horse learns only to push more on the bridle. You might have to rate your horse 150 times for him to figure out what you want, but always give him slack when he slows. Be consistent about that.

- As you rate your horse's speed, never let him get heavy on the bridle, heavy in your hands. When he pushes on the bridle, his feet can become rigid when they hit the ground. When your horse is soft in the bridle, his feet can be so soft in the ground.

- When your horse rates his speed easily in the trot, do the same things to rate his speed in the canter. First, be sure the horse's body is gathered and soft. Then pick up your reins and rate his lope. Release immediately when your horse responds.

- If your horse is pushy when you rate his canter, lope circles in a somewhat confined place. He can't get completely away from you, but you don't have to pull on his face every second. He must really work to gather his body and lope small circles, so he tires quickly. Be careful not to let your horse's inside shoulder drop into the circle. If it does, keep loping and pick up the shoulder.

- If your horse is pushy when you ask him to rate as you lope small circles, bring the horse to a stop, and then lope off in a small circle again. Repeat if necessary.

- If your horse is really on the muscle while trotting or loping in circles, flex him down to the outside of the circle with one hand to the hip, the way you learned in Chapter 6. If you must go to the hip, don't be too thoughtful about it. This should become an unconscious move when your horse pushes on your hands; you don't want him to enjoy it. After the pull to your hip, don't let your horse stay still long before you lope another circle. Standing still is fine when you ask for a nice stop and get it, but not as part of that correction.

- If your horse doesn't seem to respond at all when asked to rate, don't say whoa; just pick up one rein and pull him into the ground. Quickly bump him back a few steps before you go forward again. You might even change directions or walk forward so your horse wonders what's next. Make everything hard work when your horse is on the muscle.

The Rundown

We've all seen horses run down the arena and anticipate stops, and the stops are never pretty. To make a nice stop, a horse must be true and honest in his rundown. Once he's trained to understand the rundown and the stop, it's all about keeping him guessing so that he doesn't anticipate.

Straightness in the rundown is important. When a horse anticipates, he isn't gathered and driving into the stop, so his body isn't straight. When it's not straight, his rundown and his stop can't be straight. But both can be straight when a horse drives into the stop.

People sometimes "fence" reining horses to keep them running straight the full length of the arena. I don't do much fencing, just enough at a show for my horse to know that he can go completely to the end of the pen.

When I work on rundowns at home, I don't stop every time, but use a lot of downward transitions. Most people think those transitions could lead to my horse setting up, anticipating the stop. More than anything, those downward transitions keep him soft on the bit, flexed at the poll and in frame. At the show, he expects that change, so he's soft, and when I say whoa, he melts into the ground.

- When you can make the downward transitions for ranch riding, you have the foundation to make good rundowns. Be sure your horse is responsive in those basic transitions before you run and stop him, and expect the desired response.

- When you first drive a horse fast down the arena, he can be uncertain, sometimes looking back instead of forward. His body isn't straight and neither is the rundown. Instead of stopping your horse, do downward transitions from an extended lope to a slow lope until your horse is straight and comfortable with his speed and with checking it.

- In the rundown, your horse should be soft in hand and drive off his back end, just like he should in any gait. As you increase your speed, pick up slightly on the bridle reins to keep his front end elevated, and be sure his hind end stays gathered beneath him. That's true no matter if you ask for a complete stop or a downward transition.

- If your horse pushes against your hands as you run down the arena, bump him forward into the bridle with your legs, and block his face with your hands. Remind him to collect himself and be light. If you don't, he's too rigid to melt into the ground when you stop.

- As you gain speed in the rundown, if your horse feels rigid, probably he's flattened his spine or has lost his drive. Do a downward transition to a slow lope or a walk, and then speed up. Keep doing that until your horse softens and starts listening. When you finally ask him to stop, say whoa and move your legs out and away from his body. Because his front end and spine are soft now, he pedals right into that stop as long as you don't pull hard on his head.

- Don't stop your horse every time you make a rundown at home. Stop maybe twice, and then do a downward transition as you come to the fence. If you're in a right lead at the end, do slow down, but continue loping in a right lead around the end of the pen. Then do the same

thing at the other end of the pen and/or in the left lead. You might stop and let your horse blow at the other end or do something else. Mix up things. Otherwise, your horse gets smart and anticipates. Use those downward transitions in the mix to help soften your horse and keep his attention.

- At home, use both leads when you work on rundowns. Work on the left lead for a while and then the right. Keep your horse guessing. Most horses usually stop better on one lead than the other. It makes sense to work on both so your horse is comfortable stopping in either lead.

Rundown Showmanship

- Sometimes the versatility dry-work pattern calls for you to run your horse past a cone at the far end of the arena before you do a rollback or other maneuver. When that's the case, head your horse straight down the arena, but you might not really start accelerating until you're past the center marker.

- If the pattern doesn't call for you to ride beyond the far end marker, you might want to start accelerating before you get to the center, but not go quite so far down the pen. That way, you sometimes can find a little better ground for stopping your horse.

- Judge what your pattern tells you to do in light of what you know about your horse and how he accelerates best. Some horses accelerate better earlier in the rundown, rather than later.

- Judges don't much like it when you lope down the arena and really kick up your horse the last three strides. A gradual acceleration is better than going from first gear to fourth all at once.

- Many horses get heavier and heavier in hand because they know the rundown ends with the stop, so the rider tends to really pull on that type horse. Again, use downward transitions to keep that heaviness from becoming a real problem.

Fencing a horse teaches a horse he can go completely to the end of the pen and still make a smooth stop.

Soft Stops

Before I start working on a horse's stop, I want him a little tired. Then he's ready to listen when I ask him to stop. Anybody can gyp a horse around a pen to get off the edge, but sometimes, despite the groundwork, a horse still can be pushy when he's ridden. Fortunately, here on the ranch, when a horse is frisky, I have a lot of miles to ride and plenty to do.

- A good stop takes confidence. When you know you've prepared your horse to stop, you can relax and lope him, say whoa, and he gets in the ground.

- As you increase your speed in the rundown going into the stop, pick up slightly on the bridle reins to keep your horse's front end elevated. Be sure his hind end stays gathered underneath him. Then, just a second before you say whoa

for the stop, lower your reins. How much you lower the reins depends on the horse and how much help he needs.

- When you stop with one horse, you might lower your reins, but continue using them slightly to help keep his front end elevated as he stops. Another horse might not need steadying at all. You can just say whoa and lower your rein hand.

- Make a big point of using all three signals for a stop. The reins are one signal, the word "whoa" is the second signal, and your feet coming off your horse's sides are the third.

- You already laid the groundwork for the rein cue when you worked to develop softness and lightness in Chapter 6. By now, your horse should know a change is coming when he feels you lift the reins.

- Your horse also should really respond to the word "whoa" if you've used it consistently.

- When you trot or lope your horse, your legs move in rhythm against his sides. When you stop your horse, quit riding with your legs and bring them slightly away from his sides. You probably have been doing that, but might not really be aware of it.

- Many people don't make those stop signals completely clear to their horses. When any signal is completely clear to your horse and you use that signal consistently, your horse can learn it.

- Teach each of the three stop cues to your horse individually, not all three at the same time. Go over each signal with your horse at a walk until he understands, then at a trot, a lope and a gallop. When your horse gallops and responds to each cue, you're really prepared for stopping work and good results.

- When you're ready to stop, push your horse to the end of the rundown and have faith that he will stop. Trust your preparation, and your horse probably becomes good at stopping.

- Typical stopping mistake No. 1: You lack the confidence to drive your horse into a stop. Often a horse knows how to gather himself and drive toward a stop, but that training comes right out of him when his rider has no confidence in using it. But you can have confidence when you know that your horse is responsive and that he understands to stop. Because you're prepared, you no longer fear a stop. You have confidence you can make the stop.

- There can be other reasons a horse doesn't drive into his stop. Maybe the rider's signals aren't clear, and the horse can't read them and scotches. Or his rider's timing might be totally wrong, and the horse braces and stiffens as he stops because he's confused.

- When you say whoa and then bounce about 10 feet, it's not so much that you're tight and tense, but because you aren't driving your horse to the stop. When your horse drives with his back feet, they come farther forward underneath him. Then you say whoa, and your horse's feet are where they need to be to make and hold a soft stop.

- Many people don't even feel a horse's rhythm or have a clue when he's in the right place to stop. You can keep rhythm with your horse with your legs, pumping his feet slightly, but not kicking him. Then, as you say whoa, move your legs out and away from his sides to really help your horse stop.

- Typical stopping mistake No. 2: You stiffen your body before saying whoa. That sends the horse mixed signals, so he scotches. Then, when you do say whoa, the horse is out of position to make a nice stop. Instead, stay soft in your lower back and say whoa like you're letting out your air after a stomach crunch—"whooooaaa." Some people describe that softness in the back as getting down into the cutter's slump.

- Typical stopping mistake No. 3: You lose your focus during the rundown and stop. Showing a horse is tough. Halfway through a rundown, you might think about something that has nothing to do with the show. That's human nature. To score well in the dry work, stay focused and look ahead as you drive your horse into the stop. Usually the more you show, the better you get at maintaining your focus. Look down the arena and think, "Drive," and keep your shoulders back when you stop.

- Typical stopping mistake No. 4: Your hands move way too fast when you lose focus. You shouldn't have to stop your horse with your hands. If you must pull him into the ground with your hands, go back and train your horse to stop. Then your horse listens to whoa. He feels your back soften as you say it and your feet move away from his sides. You don't have to pull the reins because your horse understands what to do.

- All your hands should do when you say whoa is steady your horse. If he wants to bump against his bridle, that's his choice. Just be sure to use your hands on the reins to make that wall and block his face. Then drive him into the wall with your legs until he backs off the bridle. Use your hands only to create a barrier to block forward motion. Don't pull harder and harder on the reins.

The Pinch-Down

Here's something I do to help lighten my horse in the stop when he seems a little heavy in hand. Doing this also reminds my horse to round his back and flex his poll, which puts his face more on the vertical. Plus, this prepares my horse and puts him in position to back immediately after a stop.

- Ride one-handed and ask your horse to stop. Be sure to give him an opportunity to stop. If he doesn't, instead of pulling with your left rein hand, slide your right hand down the reins to pinch them off down low on your horse's neck and take out the slack. Your horse can't jerk his head away from you, and if he pushes on the reins, they pull on his neck. That's a barrier he must respect.

- When you pinch the reins, your horse stops himself more than you stop him with your left hand. He puts the pressure on himself to stay in position. Everything is where it ought to be, perfectly framed to stop. His back is round and his face is vertical with no

The pinch-down helps lighten the stop by reminding a horse to round the back and flex the poll, and also prepares a horse to back in frame after the stop.

gapping. Usually when you pull back on a horse with both hands, he gaps his mouth, and regardless of how steady you try to be with two hands, the reins and your hands are seldom even.

- If your horse continues to push on the bridle, keep your right hand on the reins at his neck and bump with your feet until he backs off the bit.

- As soon as you feel your horse stop, smooch for him to back, but be sure to stop his forward motion first. Keep your right hand pinched down on the rein as you back and, again, your horse can't get out of position.

Showmanship and Stops

Here are a few things I've learned about rundowns and stops that might help when you're showing in the versatility dry work.

- The main thing: Don't look down at the ground where you want to stop. When you plan your stop, it's human nature to look for it. When you look down, even though you think you're sitting down in your saddle, you tend to drive your horse's front end into the ground at that spot. Instead, keep your eyes focused ahead and above the arena fence, not on the ground, as you drive your horse to the spot, and when you say whoa, everything is much smoother.

- If you really ride up and kick your horse to go, you must move back in your saddle for the stop. A judge doesn't really get you for that, but your horse can't continue stopping smoothly for long because he feels you think about moving back in your saddle. He anticipates your stop, and it's not a soft slide. When you think it's time to sit back, he thinks, "I'm done." However, when you teach your horse to make smooth transitions and rate his speed, you shouldn't have to ride hard to make him go, which can interfere with a nice stop.

- Sit down on your horse as you drive him with your feet almost at the front cinch toward the stop. Work with your horse at home so he understands that both your

Use all three signals for a stop. The reins and the word "whoa" are two signals. Your feet coming off the horse's sides are the third.

legs can drive him while you're sitting down in the saddle.

- Slide plates aren't a necessity for our versatility reining yet, and much of the time, the arena ground isn't very good for stopping. For now, when a horse stops in frame and drops his butt in a 5- or 10-foot slide, everybody's happy.

The "Get-Back"

More than anything, when I back my horse, I want him to back more off my feet and body motion than off my hands. I also want him to move quickly and back freely. I don't want to pull him back with my reins; that doesn't look pretty to a judge.

The other thing about backing is that it's so good for my horse's stops. Backing strengthens the same muscles he needs for stopping. That's why I pay as much attention to backing my horse as I do to stopping him, to build that muscle memory.

When a horse develops a free-moving back-up, he also develops the muscle strength and body position necessary for stopping.

A horse that understands the "get-back" learns to automatically square his feet and balance himself in preparation for another maneuver.

- When you quit worrying about the stop and think about the back that follows, the stop will come. That's because your horse has learned the back is coming and positions himself for it, which is right where he needs to be for a nice stop.

- When you say whoa, your horse must not only stop, but also stop and learn to get back. Work on the "get-back" as much or more than you do the stop. Think of your horse going back immediately almost as an extension of your stop. Then he's positioned and ready for either.

- If your horse has a hard time backing, don't pull and pull on the reins. Review the backing section material in Chapter 8. Remember to block your horse's forward motion with your hands and hold. Use your feet to make your horse's feet move and smooch to him. Be patient until he steps back. Then release him.

- Even though your horse already might back easily, you now need to step up the pace. When you stop and immediately ask him to back, he learns to back fast. Gradually ask for speed as you back him and use your feet, but always keep the stop and the back smooth, soft and light.

- When backing your horse, keep him invigorated, not so much with your hands, but with your legs and by smooching to him. Then he learns what you want and knows to back quickly with a smooch.

- Done right, a horse backs without the rider using the bridle. That's what works about doing the stop with the immediate get-back. It really livens up a horse's response, and he learns how to speed up as he backs. Then he flies back and stands quietly when you release him. That's when you impress a judge.

- If your horse is crooked as he backs, review the body control exercises in Chapter 7. Then drop your leg back and along his side to straighten him easily.

- If you have taught a horse to back step-by-step, he should come around. But you must be careful with a highly resistant horse because he could come over backward with you. You must have the feel and timing to know when that can happen. If you don't, you're in a dangerous place and need professional help. Always get help whenever you need it.

Practice the moves you and your horse need to make a lead change until you're comfortable doing them before you canter through the maneuver.

11

CIRCLES AND LEAD CHANGES

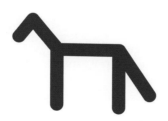

Making a lead change is like doing a nice spin; the rider must have in mind what he really wants his horse to do. So often a person drives a horse's front end into the change, and hopes the back end follows, but the rider's never sure of the response he might get. He doesn't really know what his horse must do during the lead change, and he can't really know that until he understands how his horse's body moves to make the change. A rider who knows what his horse must do can help his horse through the change.

I seldom have trouble now with lead changes, but, boy, I used to. Then I started doing things the way I describe below. It just makes sense that when my horse is in the left lead and I want to change to the right, his right shoulder needs to be up. When

the right shoulder drops, he can't make the change. When I pick up that shoulder and move his hip, a lead change can be so pretty.

To many people, a lead change seems to be a difficult, big maneuver. It's not. Like any other advanced maneuver, a lead change is simply a combination of basic things. Elevating your horse's shoulder and moving his hip are the two basic moves you need to change leads, in addition to the lightness and collection you want with any maneuver.

A controlled, easy change is your big pay-off for taking the time to teach your horse the basics. Otherwise, you're just riding a fast horse that's pulling on your hands. When you can ride at a fast clip and rate and move your horse, a lead change is easy.

When the horse's feet hit the ground, he'll be in the right lead. Knowing the footfall of a horse's canter is a big help in understanding leads and changes.

The Performance Goal

The lead change is simply the next step in your riding program, one you've prepared yourself and your horse to take. You've built the foundation for the change. Now all you do is combine those basic maneuvers in a specific way. And, no, you and your horse probably aren't entirely comfortable with that at first, but you soon can be because you can practice those combinations at a walk or trot. Then, when you canter, the change is smooth and quiet.

A lead change makes ranch work easy when a cow changes directions in the pasture, the same as it makes reining work easy in a versatility class. You and your horse can make that change and stay in balance. More than anything, changing leads builds your confidence so much because you and your horse really learn to communicate to perform the maneuver.

Review Your Skills

It might seem redundant to keep reviewing the same basic skills when you warm up your horse, but it's important to do that. One skill builds on another, and each advanced maneuver is a combination of the basic skills. Checking your horse's response in the warm-up is how you develop your timing, your feel for your horse, and how you keep a small problem from becoming a big one.

The Circles

Riders and their horses sometimes get lost going from small, slow circles to large, fast ones, or vice versa, and speed can blow their minds. So you work on those transitions at home to build your control.

You must be clear and consistent with your horse, especially when you add speed to anything, to help your horse stay out of trouble and find the comfort zone. Then he can give you what you want, and you really are able to gain confidence in your control.

When you lope circles, having control during the transitions in speed and size helps set up your horse for smooth lead changes and a good score in the versatility dry work. You also build in the control you need when your horse must move fast to keep up with a cow in the roping or cutting.

Control isn't repeatedly picking on a horse's mouth. He doesn't understand a thing and gets hard-mouthed because he's trying to bear the aggravation or pain. There is no opportunity for him to find relief. That relief is the comfort zone a horse gets when he does what his rider wants.

Control isn't letting a horse do what he wants either. I don't want to be forceful with a horse, but I do put restraints on him. That's what my bridle and feet are. He learns what to do by the way I move my body, and when he responds, he finds that comfort zone. If a horse doesn't respond, he learns that something more severe is coming. Horses are smart, and most horses want to stay out of trouble.

Here are a few ways you can help your horse find his comfort zone when he lopes circles and makes changes in their size and speed without any problems.

- Most people don't work with speed very often. That can get you in trouble in the show arena. When your horse goes wide open in a cattle class or a reining pattern, he's lost. He doesn't know how to do what you want at 90 miles an hour.

- Riders often overlook teaching a horse how to run fast, and then get scared when the horse doesn't know how to handle his feet and run. You must get your horse broke for speed, just like you teach him to turn around or stop. Add speed gradually at home. Then your horse can figure out to keep coming back to you, and you have control.

- Adding speed shouldn't be a problem when your horse is soft and light, and you can elevate his forehand. By now, he should know how to flex his poll, round his back and keep his balance. All he needs to learn is to do these things while going fast.

- Before you really ask your horse for speed, test his basic downward transitions at a trot and a lope. Ask him to go a little faster, and then ask him to rate back his speed. If he doesn't, make him come back to you. Stick him in the ground, if necessary, to get his attention.

- If you must take drastic measures to maintain control when you lope your horse, work on the warm-up exercises for softness and lightness before you try

Using cones at home is one way to learn to lope a circle and to develop control in the size and speed transitions between small, slow and large, fast circles.

more high-speed transitions. Your horse must learn that he slows down when you ask. Improving downward transitions can help everything from a rollback or stop to collection. There's nothing quite like picking up your hand and feeling your horse melt.

- Don't expect your horse to rate back from high speed in two strides; it might take three or more for him to do that. The faster he goes, the more strides it takes, but as long as he's soft in your hands and trying to respond, give him time to figure out that's what you want. Once your horse learns to make transitions with real speed, he often becomes lighter than he was before the fast work. As you build speed, work to maintain that light response.

- Work with your horse at home so that you also are comfortable changing the size of your circles and can keep them round. In versatility dry work, certain size circles must be ridden in specific areas of the arena. Loping an egg here, instead of a round circle, can throw you off over there, later in the pattern. The goal is for your circles to be placed in an arena just like they look in the pattern diagram.

- There's only one way to learn to make nice, round circles, and that's to ride your horse in circles. You don't have to run your horse out of air to do that either; you can learn to ride a round circle at a trot before you pick up speed. Ride circles until you know yours are round.

- To learn to ride round circles, set up four cones in a square and circle them horseback. Or set up one cone as the center of an imaginary circle and practice until you're confident you can ride a round circle around the cone.

- If your horse's tracks show in your arena dirt, make a round circle and follow the tracks until you learn to stay on the circle. Then move 10 or 20 feet outside that circle and make more tracks for your large circles.

- Making nice circles takes riding time but isn't difficult to do. Don't worry about speed in your circles until you have the shape down.

- Don't always ride from the same small, slow circles to the same large, fast circles in the same place each day. Your horse can learn the pattern. Always keep him gathered and framed, but mix up things. Lope a small, slow circle in one corner, a large, fast one, and then go down the arena and change your speed before you lope another circle. Then lope diagonally across the pen and change your speed again. That's taking control of your horse, and there's no pattern to it. That's probably more interesting for your horse, too.

- You can work to improve your circles at the same time you work on the downward transitions for speed control, but don't combine the two until you have the basics of each solid.

Prepare for the Lead Change

A lead change is no big deal, but it's so easy for a horse and rider to get uptight about making that transition. Remember: Those basic exercises in the review have prepared you and your horse to change leads.

When you lope down the fence and pick up a shoulder or move a hip, you're doing exactly what you do when you ask for the lead change. When you teach your horse to do these things, you teach yourself to do them, too. You can practice moving your horse's hips and shoulders at a walk, trot or lope, and those exercises work on a green colt, as well as a finished horse.

I don't work much at all on lead changes at home. Sometimes a horse can get cranky, maybe because the change scares him, and the change scares most people, too. But loping in a circle or a line and asking a horse to move his hip or pick up his shoulder doesn't bother him, and I do a lot of that without asking for a change.

You can, too. You can go through the motions, but never really ask for the change. Get those basics. Pick up your horse's shoulders and move his hips until you program yourself and your horse to make all the right moves, and you both are comfortable with the moves required to make the change.

- Before you actually change leads, you should be able to lope your horse in circles of different sizes and control his speed from almost a run. Know that you have control. Then you can concentrate on the lead change moves and not worry about how round a circle is or if your horse can rate.

- Be sure your horse is comfortable moving his shoulders on and off the arc of the circle and hingeing, or flexing, to the right and left when you lope him in a circle in either direction.

- Be sure that your horse is comfortable moving his hips when he lopes in a straight line and a circle. Moving his hips can be hard for a horse and aggravating when he's asked to do that again and again. Work in small increments rather than one long session. Be aware of your horse's tolerance; otherwise, he might start working his tail.

- Before you ever try a lead change at a lope, your horse should be able to do this exercise at a walk and a trot. Travel down the middle of the pen or on the diagonal from one corner of the arena to the other. Pick up your horse's left shoulder and arc his face to the left, too. Then put your right leg on him at about the flank cinch and push his hips to the left. When he responds, release your hand and leg, and let your horse relax. Ask your horse to do that on the same side four or five times. Then work on the other side. It's not good to switch directions every time. When your horse

Prepare for a lead change and build the muscle memory necessary to make one by picking up a horse's right shoulder and moving the hip right, at first at a walk and trot, and later in the lope.

Practice elevating the horse's left shoulder and moving his hip to the left, just as you do to the right, so you and your horse are comfortable working the lead-change basics in either direction.

is really comfortable doing that in each direction, without being antsy, a lead change comes easy.

Make the Change

Although I don't change leads a lot on my horses, here's how I make a change at home. I usually move the shoulder and hip on one side as described in the section above, and then change the lead. Then I move the shoulder and hip on the other side before I change leads again, and I don't worry too much about changing leads perfectly when I do that at home.

Because people are a little scared of lead changes, they often lean or kick at the wrong place and/or at the wrong time. Many riders have been told what to do during a change, but don't understand why. Other riders might understand what to do, but like a young horse, don't have enough experience to do those things automatically. When a rider hasn't done his homework, it's no surprise his horse doesn't understand.

So ride your horse. Get comfortable moving his hips and shoulders as you go through the motions. When they're automatic, you set yourself and your horse up to make a successful lead change.

- The big thing about a lead change is getting your horse to understand what you want him to do. After that, everything else is just timing, and changing leads becomes easier and easier for you and your horse. If your horse doesn't switch leads today, he probably will tomorrow or the next day. When the basics are correct, he can figure out the change with time.

- It's best to work slowly when you build the lead change. Then whatever the speed, your horse can make the change and remain collected and gathered.

- Moving your horse's shoulder and hip a time or two at a walk or trot, as described in the previous section, doesn't mean you're ready for a lead change. When you try one then, you put too much pressure on your horse, and that's what he remembers about the lead change—the pressure. You basically set yourself up to fail when you push yourself and your horse into doing something neither of you is comfortable doing.

- Typically, if your horse is in the left lead, your right foot is back a little on your horse's side. When you need to go faster, that's where you bump up your horse's speed. By keeping your foot back toward your horse's hip until you're ready to change leads, you help hold your horse on his circle.

- Always changing leads across the "D," the center of a figure eight, like you do in the versatility class, can become a pattern your horse learns. Good horses are smart, so do something different. When you change leads on the diagonal, from one corner of the pen to another, you teach your horse to change on a straight line, so the D at the show isn't a maneuver he anticipates.

- When you're ready to change leads, lope several circles in the left lead, for example. Leave the circles to ride on the diagonal across your pen. Then pick up your horse's right shoulder and move his hip to the right. There's the lead change. You simply go through the same motions you used earlier at a walk and trot. Those

slow motions help keep your horse quiet when you add speed.

- When you make the change from a left lead to the right, or vice versa, look up where you are going, not down into the circle. If you look down, your hand drops, which allows your horse to drop his shoulder into the ground. He can't stay elevated and drive off his hindquarters for a clean change when you look down.

- When you go from a left to a right lead, for example, put a bit of your weight onto your left pocket. Then with your right leg, open the gate so your horse has a place to go—to the right. You don't want any of your weight on the right shoulder when going to the right lead, or vice versa. When your horse has to catch your weight on the left, he can't drop to the right. But if you lean right and into the change, your horse must catch your weight on his right side, and that messes up the change. Even when you do the exercise to move your horse's hip, put weight on your outside pocket as you push his hip each way.

- After you make the change from left to right, lope around the pen or in circles and always hold up your horse's right shoulder for half to three-quarters of the way around the next circle, just to keep that shoulder to the outside and out of the way. When you change leads from right to left, do the same with your horse's left shoulder.

- After changing leads, you might even pick up your horse's shoulder or move his hip to the right. You don't change his lead, but go through the motions to be sure your horse understands.

- If you don't make a big deal of a lead change, your horse never will. If you make an issue of it when your horse doesn't switch leads at first, a lead change always is an issue.

- If your horse doesn't change clean at first, try the fixes mentioned below to help your horse figure out what he's supposed to do. Changing leads is no big deal; if your horse doesn't switch today, he probably can tomorrow or the next

When your horse is light on the bit and softly in frame as he lopes on the left lead, as shown here, as well as the right lead—and does those things consistently—he's ready to learn about changing leads.

day. When the basics are correct, he can figure out the change. The more solid he is in his basic maneuvers, the better your results when you combine the basics for advanced moves.

- If the lead change doesn't happen the first time you ask, don't bother your horse about it. Just take off the pressure to change for a few strides, then put it back on again and lift his shoulder and move his hip again.

- If your horse doesn't change the lead, you might break to a trot for one stride and cue him for the correct lead so he

understands what you want. Don't trot long because you don't want your horse to make a habit of that.

- If your horse doesn't change leads, make sure that you can pick up his shoulder and move it out of the way, that you can move his hip over to the side, and that he stays collected.

- Try going a little faster a time or two to help your horse figure out what he's supposed to do. Most horses can change leads easily with speed, but you must keep your horse from dropping his shoulder when you increase the speed.

When you and your horse understand the basics—softness, lightness and body control—it's easy to look ahead and keep your horse's front end elevated for the change, no matter if he's loping on the right lead, as shown here, or his left.

Otherwise, he might crossfire and drag his back lead.

- When you elevate your horse's shoulder, don't jerk or saw on his mouth. Pick up and hold, and be sure he drives off his back end. By now, he should understand how to hold that collected position. If he pushes against your hands, make the same correction you do in the warm-up—drive him into the bridle with your feet. When pressure on your hands stops, release the pressure from your feet.

- When your or your horse anticipates a lead change, it can become a race. Keep your horse's shoulder elevated, so he can't anticipate, flatten his spine, drop his shoulder and try to beat you going into the next lead change.

- If your versatility horse is an old veteran and has learned how to drop his shoulder, he might change leads on his front end, but drag the back lead and not change there. Go back to the basics and learn how to pick up that horse's shoulder and move his hips.

- A rider who's scared of a lead change sometimes picks up so much on the reins that his horse can't move freely or softly, and wrings his tail. He knows a change is coming and he feels how nervous his rider is. The best thing in that situation is to go back and gain some softness and confidence in each other, so you don't dread the change.

- If you simply cannot get a lead change, don't let your horse get tight and hot or fight with him. Find help before things get to that point. A horse can be ruined so quickly on a lead change, but it's something every horse can do so naturally.

Circle and Change with Style

- Look at the arena and see where the cones or markers are. Go through that reining pattern in your mind and know where your horse's circles and lead changes should be in relation to those markers.

- In the versatility dry work, don't give away points in your score when you lope circles. Know that you can lope round circles at the required speeds, and know that your circles are right on target with the pattern markers. Balance your circles on one end of the arena with those on the other end, and balance them from one side of the pen to the other, too. Be right on target when you perform each maneuver.

- There's a difference between training your horse and showing your horse. At home, you might change leads in a straight line or on the diagonal in your pen. In the versatility arena, ride the figure eight as if two "Ds" are joined in the middle. Come straight across the center of the Ds to make your lead change on target.

- At the show be right on the center marker when you make the change and balance your circle on one end of the eight with the circle on the other.

- As you make your lead change, look ahead to the next point where you want to go. Keeping your eyes up and looking ahead helps you keep your horse's shoulder elevated during the change.

- Speeding up as you come across to make a lead change doesn't raise your versatility dry work score. Your horse should never change pace, no matter what he's doing, unless the pattern calls for that change in speed.

A great trail score always comes down to control and maneuverability.

12

RANCH TRAIL

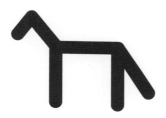

The ranch versatility trail course is designed to show a horse's willingness to deal with obstacles that often are part of daily ranch work. Usually the course has a minimum of six obstacles. In American Quarter Horse Association classes, for example, mandatory obstacles include working a gate, dismounting and mounting the horse, and dragging a log. Optional obstacles can include a water hazard, hobbling or ground-tying a horse, crossing a bridge, roping a dummy and more, and a combination of obstacles is allowed.

Versatility trail obstacles should be as natural and realistic as possible, and the course can be set up outside the arena to use the natural terrain. The trail course is different at each show, depending on the particular association's rules, but the pattern is posted for competitors before the class begins. When a horse is controllable, quiet and maneuverable, he usually does fine.

Riding through trail obstacles is not a speed event. For a long time, I thought the faster I went through the obstacles, the sooner I'd be done. I know better now. Riding through a trail course thoughtfully is another way I can show a judge what my horse can do, so now I take my time.

I deal with the same type of obstacles working cattle here on the ranch, but I'm not trying to make a world-class trail horse. I'm just trying to get my work done, and I want a quiet, manageable horse to ride when I work.

The Performance Goal

Getting a good trail class score is like scoring high in any part of the versatility. It all comes down to having control of your horse. You must ride and gather your horse to maneuver through the obstacles and instill the confidence in your horse to trust you, no matter what you face.

Riding through a trail course thoughtfully is the best way to show the judge how quiet and manageable your horse can be.

Successfully completing a versatility trail course is an issue of trust. Each time you and your horse deal with an obstacle, you build confidence in each other. You become sure of each other and rely on one another—that's trust. That trust affects not only your trail class score, but also carries over to everything you and your horse do.

Review Your Skills

Don't forget to take the edge off your horse, especially when you plan to do quiet, precise work like that in a trail class. The flexion and body-control exercises from the previous chapters make a really good warm-up for working on trail obstacles. See the complete list of exercises with chapter references at the back of the book.

The Posted Pattern

Look closely at the versatility trail pattern when it's posted at a show. The pattern shows the order you ride through the obstacles and also which gaits you use when you're between obstacles.

The trail course used in this chapter is just an example of a pattern you might find posted when you compete in ranch versatility. The pattern includes the three mandatory obstacles and optional ones, with ideas

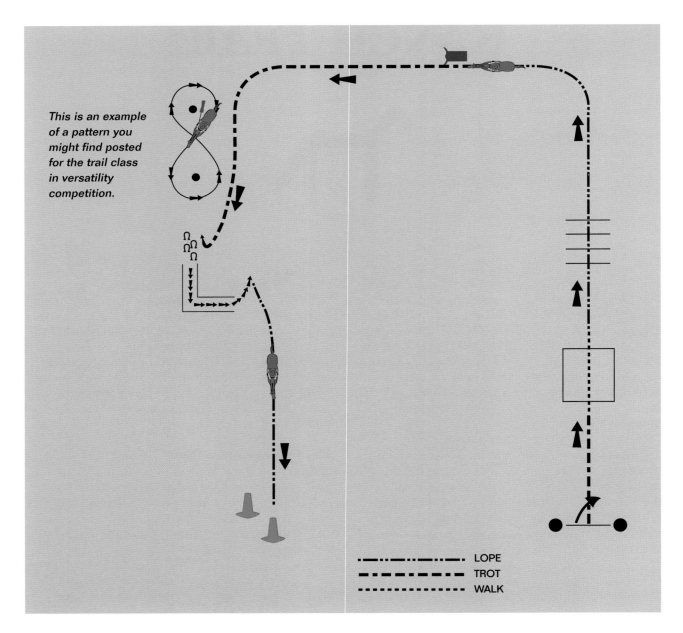

This is an example of a pattern you might find posted for the trail class in versatility competition.

LOPE
TROT
WALK

about how best to approach each obstacle and make transitions between them. You can use an approach similar to the ones described here on almost any obstacle to continue building your horse's trust.

Work the Gate

The approach to an obstacle often can be as important as completing the obstacle itself. Some horses are so pumped when they come to the arena to work the gate. Usually the rider has just tried something in the warm-up pen, like a side-pass, but the horse has no idea what to do. So he's uptight, sometimes from dodging a spur.

Don't leave your best performance in the practice pen or ask your horse for something he doesn't understand. His skills are right where they were when you left home, and the warm-up pen isn't the place to teach something new. Take a quiet, calm approach to keep your horse as comfortable and smooth

as possible when you approach and work the gate or any obstacle.

- To work the gate, you must be able to move your horse's front end and back end, and side-pass. In the warm-up pen you might quietly ask him to do these things to review what he knows before you enter the arena, but you build those skills at home when there's no pressure on your horse.

- At home, walk to the gate and let your horse stand there until he's comfortable and relaxed so he can be that way at a show, too. Only then do you actually go to work and open the gate.

- Whatever hand you have on the reins when you walk into the show arena is the hand you have on the reins when

Quietly working a gate at home uses and reinforces basic body control as a horse moves his shoulders, hips and rib cage to maneuver through the obstacle.

you leave the arena. You must use that hand throughout the pattern, but you can switch hands when an obstacle requires that. If you switch at a show, be sure to switch back to your normal rein hand before riding to the next obstacle. Practice switching your rein hand at home so you can do it smoothly at the show with no problem.

- The gate in the photos and diagram is a right-hand push gate. In other words, you must push it open before riding your horse through.

- A left-handed gate can be difficult to work when you ride with your reins in your left hand, or vice versa. To push the gate, you must swap the reins to your other hand and make that change before you touch the obstacle. Approach the gate with the reins in your normal riding hand and wait for the judge to nod. When he does, switch the reins to your other hand, if necessary, before you side-pass to the gate and open it. Only when you have latched the gate and completely finish working the obstacle should you switch back to your normal rein hand.

- Some people ride up to and alongside the gate in the approach, but this is versatility competition, so show what your horse can do. Side-pass him to the gate with his head toward the opening to demonstrate your control, and then unlatch the gate. Once you put your hand on the gate, don't take it off the gate—ever—until you're done.

- With your hand in the middle of the gate, push it open wide enough that your horse has room to go through the opening. Ride through and be very aware of your horse's head, shoulders and hips. If you bump the gate, the judge can take a deduction. Be smooth and natural at the gate, and don't get strung out, leaning way over to hold onto it.

- As you ride through the gate, slide your hand to the end, where you turn the horse to allow him to go through that opening. When your leg is at the end of a gate, ask your horse to come around the end. He basically pivots around your leg,

and when he completes his turn, your leg still should be at the end of the gate, just on the other side of it.

- When you close the gate, again, stay aware of your horse's hips. They must be completely clear of the gate. Only then do you side-pass your horse to shut the gate. Don't get in a hurry and bump it.

- After you push the gate closed, latch it if the pattern requires you to do that.

Showmanship at the Gate

- If you don't have the control to side-pass your horse to the gate and/or to stop him before he bumps it, don't show the judge what your horse can't do. A judge docks you for that. Instead, just walk your horse up to and alongside the gate to open it.

- When you complete the gate work, always side-pass your horse maybe two steps out and away from the gate, again, to show your control. Then turn him in the direction of the next obstacle.

Cross the Bridge

The transition: After you leave the gate, trot to the bridge as shown in the pattern. Make the downward transition to break into a walk a few steps from the bridge. Trotting right to the bridge and asking a horse to step onto it is too much for most horses, so establish the walk before your horse steps onto the obstacle.

- In your approach, if your horse drops his head to look at the bridge, that's great. It shows that he's aware of it.

- Hit that bridge dead-center in your approach. Otherwise, your horse might try to walk off the outside edge.

- If you build a practice bridge at home, make sure it can hold your horse's weight. You could put a piece of plywood on the ground, to accustom your horse to that different sound of walking on wood, but the step-up is what bothers most horses, so a bridge works best.

Always be sure your practice bridge is sturdy enough to hold a horse's weight.

- Some bridges are built in a sloping arch from the ground, rather than as a step-up. If your practice bridge is a step-up, your horse might have a little trouble with the arched bridge. Horses tend to stumble on that because that arch is an optical illusion to them, and they don't realize the slope is there.

- If you have trouble getting your horse to cross a bridge, try putting your bridge in the round pen and at first let your horse travel to the side of it. Then gradually move the bridge until it's right in your horse's path of travel. This same approach works to get a horse used to a tarp, too. The main thing: Build your horse's trust so he doesn't worry and goes where you want.

- Another approach to get your horse comfortable with a bridge is to put it about 2 feet from your arena fence.

Rather than fight with your horse or spend a lot of time, ride your horse between the fence and the bridge as you work him. Just make the bridge part of his scenery. When he travels beside it easily, stop and put him across the bridge—not the length of it, the width. That's the most he has to do at first. After that, it seldom takes much more for him to handle the length of the bridge.

- A bridge is no problem unless you want to make it one. If your horse is scared of a bridge, or any obstacle, outthink him beforehand. Don't cram the obstacle down his throat. Figure out a way to make your horse understand and learn that the obstacle can't hurt him. Once he's crossed a bridge a time or two, you can change your approach or move the bridge wherever you want it.

Lope-Overs

The transition: After your horse steps off that bridge, make a smooth transition into the left lead that's called for in the pattern. Approaching the lope-over poles is similar to approaching a bridge. Use good showmanship and line up your horse dead-center in the middle of the poles and keep him collected.

- The versatility trail pattern can include walk- and trot-overs in addition to lope-overs. So you must know how the poles are set up at a show, and how your horse handles a 7-foot lope-over as compared with a 6-foot one, which depends on his size and his collection.

- Use the AQHA rules as a guideline to set up practice poles at home. For walkovers, set the poles 20 to 24 inches apart and at least 22 inches if poles are elevated. For trot-overs, set the poles 3 feet to 3 feet, 6 inches apart, and lope-over poles should be 6 to 7 feet apart.

- When you practice on the poles at home, count your horse's rhythm—1, 2, 3 for the lope and 1, 2 for the trot. That steady rhythm is especially helpful if riding over the poles is new to you or your horse.

- Set up your horse for whatever he must do. If it's a 7-foot lope-over, for example,

Use the American Quarter Horse Association guidelines to determine the correct spacing for practicing walk-, trot-, and lope-overs at home.

and you have a 14-hand horse, let him extend his stride. If you have a big horse and a 6-foot lope-over, you must gather him to get through the poles. Lope over a lot of poles to get a feel for how your horse strides through them. Adjusting your horse's stride through the poles is similar to a jumper adjusting his horse's stride so his timing is good.

- Gather your horse so he drives off his back end and stays off the bridle, just like you do in the warm-up. Collection counts in the lope-overs because you can lose a half-point for a tick, or slightly touching a pole, and 1 point for hitting a pole, not just bumping it.

- If your horse bumps poles at home, try setting them a few inches off the ground to get him to pay attention. You might set two long poles parallel with the lope-over poles on top. A horse is smart and

soon learns when poles are elevated. When you put the poles back on the ground, if he's lazy-footed, he probably starts shuffling his feet again. That's why teaching him to gather and really drive off his back end is important.

- At home, to help gather your horse as he lopes over the poles, fan the poles out from the center of an imaginary circle lengthwise to the circle's arc. With the poles fanned, you can pick the distance between them to use. How much your horse must lengthen or shorten his stride depends on where you approach each pole—near the center of the circle or close to the edge.

Showmanship Over the Poles

- As you ride through the poles at a show, don't look down; look beyond them, where you want your horse to go. That helps maintain his collection and keeps you on track with the pattern

- Keep your horse gathered a few strides after he crosses the last pole. Otherwise, he might relax, flatten his back and drop a foot before he's beyond the last pole. Not allowing that to happen is showmanship, and if you plan for that at home, your horse is okay with that at the show and doesn't tick a pole.

- Should the trail pattern, for example, call for you to lope over poles and then trot, don't stop; make a downward transition. When your horse is collected, he's in frame for the transition.

- If the pattern doesn't call for a stop, but a rider stops anyway, a judge could see that as breaking the pattern, as a disqualification, or as a break of gait. Do exactly what the posted pattern requires.

Rope the Dummy

The transition: Don't let your horse flatten his back and string out after he leaves the poles. The pattern calls for you to lope to another obstacle, the roping dummy, so keep your horse gathered in a nice canter in the correct lead.

- As you approach the dummy, stop your horse right where you want to be when you rope the dummy. It's best that you don't stop and then reposition your horse on the dummy.

- When you rope right-handed, and a hay bale is the dummy, line up the outside of your right leg with the dummy's left side. The point of your horse's right shoulder should be right off the bale's back left corner. Depending on how you like to rope, the best position is 6 inches forward or back from there and/or a few more inches to the side.

- Don't spend a lot of time getting your rope ready to use. There might be 30 or 40 more people to go. Stop your horse, get your rope and build your loop quickly, but not so fast that you mess up handling your rope.

Work at home until you can ride your horse right to the roping position you prefer and then know that he'll stand quietly at the dummy while you rope.

- At the dummy, your horse should stand quietly on a loose rein, no matter what you do with your rope. Work with him at home until he's totally comfortable standing still at the dummy.

- You should be able to catch the dummy, but if you don't, it's not the end of the world. Usually there is no penalty if you miss when you rope an obstacle.

- For more on roping a dummy and handling a rope safely, see the next chapter.

Showmanship at the Dummy

- Know your horse. Your horse really ought to be broke enough to lope to the dummy and stop softly right where he needs to be. If he's a little flighty, you might have to change the ideal approach to the dummy to keep your horse from spooking. Then it's best to stop and walk him into position.

- The judge looks for a quiet, relaxed horse standing still on a loose rein. If your horse is antsy or chomping at the bit, you might be marked down on this maneuver.

- Once you've built your loop with your horse standing quietly, you might pick up his head slightly right before you rope so the judge sees your horse's alertness.

- Some people rope the dummy, back the horse, and even throw the slack. Do just what the posted pattern says and not anything more.

- After you rope, do you leave the rope on the ground or coil it? Usually you are given an opportunity to ask the judge. One judge might say to get the rope off the dummy if you can, but another one is okay with you throwing the rope on the ground and going to the next obstacle. Still another might want you to get your rope, even if you have to get off the horse to do that.

- Always ask if you can ride up beside the dummy to pull off your rope. Most judges are fine with that. If you think your horse might be a little scared or uneasy with that, and the judge says it's okay to drop the rope, just drop it. Otherwise, you take a chance on losing points. Again, show what your horse has, not what he doesn't have. Don't try to showboat and make your horse look lacking in his skills.

Drag the Log

The transition: When you complete the dummy obstacle and are coiling your rope, but must go to the next obstacle in a trot, be really aware of your leg cues. If you cue with only one foot, and your horse is attentive, he could break into a lope. In this pattern, your horse should trot right from a standstill toward the log drag.

- Always tighten your cinch before the versatility trail class. You could get in trouble dragging the log. At shows, there's a tendency to use big, heavy logs that really test horses, so be sure your cinch is tight enough to handle the pull.

- Anytime you must pull something, use a breast collar on your horse. Then the weight doesn't pull the saddle back over your horse's loins or sideways. Some horses blow up when that happens.

- When you ride to the log drag, try to stop so that the rope around the drag is right by your horse. Then you can side-pass over to pick up the rope.

- Usually the rope is on a stand or a barrel and has been left with kinks in it and hung any ol' way. Pick up the rope and get out the kinks first. There's no deduction for coiling the rope correctly. A judge might not plus you for it, but should think more of you for doing that. When your horse stands quietly while you handle the rope, you demonstrate your control.

- Always line up the rope coils smoothly in your hand. If you get in a wreck and have to let coils go, you can open your hand and easily drop a coil.

- Lift up the rope and keep it taut between you and the drag before you go to your horn to dally.

- When you dally, bring the rope around the front of your horn from right to left, or counterclockwise. Then go back around again to make one full wrap on your horn. Keep your right thumb up and out of your rope as you dally it.

- As you start to drag the log, remember that it represents a cow, so handle the rope like there's a real cow on the end of it. Hold up the rope and keep it off the ground as much as you can; that's kind of a cowboy rule. Also keep the rope up and away from your horse's feet. Otherwise, the "cow" could run up and over the rope, or your horse might step across it. Either is an absolute wreck.

Handle your rope like there's a real cow on the end of it and keep the rope up and away from your horse's feet.

- With the coils placed correctly in your hand, you can help keep your horse out of trouble. If, by chance, the rope is so tight that the log bumps your horse's back feet, drop a coil and let the rope slide around your horn to give your horse some relief. Keep about a horse-length distance between your horse and the log.

- Most versatility patterns require you to drag the log in a figure eight, which means you must change directions. When you do, the log goes right behind your horse. The rope should go over the horse's rump, not under his tail or down by his hocks and legs. If necessary, slide your hand back to help pick up the rope. There's no deduction for helping your horse then.

- If you have a too-short rope in the crossover, the rope can get down around your horse's hips. If it does and the log represents a 600-pound calf, it's too close. Your horse wouldn't be able to pull the calf. So feed a little rope around your saddle horn—as long as you can do

it without getting a coil stuck there. The extra length gives your horse a bit more working advantage.

- When you start dragging the log, maintain forward motion to keep everything smooth. Don't stop halfway through the eight unless your horse gets in too big a rush, and you must stop and fix that.

- Make sure your circles in the eight are big enough that the log, as you drag it, doesn't hit anything, the rope stand, for example.

- As you end the drag, try to come back to the exact place you started. The log should be where it was when you rode to it, and your horse should be lined up with the stand where you hang the rope.

- If you must go past the stand a step or two to put the log where you want it, do that. Then stop and back your horse until you're directly across from the rope stand and can side-pass to it.

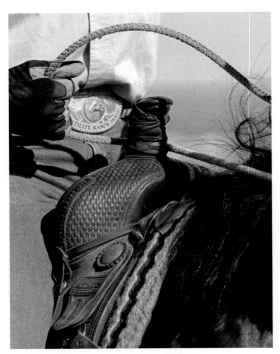

Be mindful of safety when you dally your rope, and be sure the coils are lined up smoothly in your left hand.

- When you put the rope on the stand, be sure the rope end toward the log is away from your horse's feet. Otherwise, he could step over the rope or when you hang up the rope, it could come up between your horse's legs. Always be aware of that rope in relation to his legs.

- For more information on safely dallying a rope, see the next chapter.

Showmanship and the Log Drag

- During the log drag, most judges want to see how well your horse handles the rope crossing over his butt during the figure eight. Prepare him for that at home so that he's totally comfortable no matter where the rope touches him.

- Some trail patterns call for you to face the log and back your horse at the end of a log drag, but not all do. Some judges might be okay with you trying to do and show more than the pattern requires, but not all judges are. If the pattern calls for you to face and back, do that; if not, don't do anything more.

- Switching hands on the reins during the log drag is similar to switching hands when you work the gate. You must commit and switch that hand before you start the obstacle, and then you must go back to that original rein hand when you're done.

Back Through the "L"

The transition: When you leave the log drag, make a quarter-pivot before you head to the "L" back-through. That pivot gives a sharpness and crispness to the way you approach the back-through. Trot from the log drag to the back-through.

- How you approach the L depends on what the pattern requires. One pattern might call for you to ride through the L and then back through it. This pattern calls for you to ride to the L, reverse your horse and then back through the L.

- This pattern doesn't require you to turn a particular direction before you back through the L. When the judge doesn't specify the direction, rein your horse the way he usually turns best.

- Walk your horse head-on to the L, stop and then pivot him on his back end. After he turns, his back end should be lined up with the L. That's being on target.

- If your horse tends to be a little edgy, now is the time to slow him down. Let him stand a second or two before you start backing. Remember: There's no time clock on you here.

- People often get antsy backing through the L, and that nervousness feeds down into their horses. If your horse begins to seem a little antsy, recognize the pressure on him. There's pressure from both your legs, and pressure to stop really quick if he takes a wrong step to one side or the other. When any horse backs, he tends to get on the muscle faster than he does going forward. Take a deep breath and try to be quiet and easy when you back your horse, and be precise when you do.

- At first, it's hard for a young horse, or any horse, to back smoothly and fluidly

Know how the posted trail pattern calls for you to approach the "L" and if it's set up with an adjacent box.

through the corner of the L although most get better as they mature and learn. If you must, hesitate a second to move your horse's hip over one step in the corner before you start backing again. Go for that fluid move through the corner when your horse isn't ready for that, and he can get antsy and might hit a pole. Taking that second to move his hip is better that hitting the pole.

- If you feel your horse get tight as you back through the L, let him flatten his back a little and then move his hip through the corner, rather than trying to back and move his hip at the same time. That takes some pressure off him.

- Sometimes the L can be set up as part of a box. Usually you trot over the logs on the inside of the L and then back through the L from the other end. When you're done, you walk over the logs to the next obstacle.

- You might even have to trot into the box and then spin your horse two circles each way. Whatever the pattern calls for, set up your horse correctly for each maneuver and take it slow and easy.

Dismount and Mount

The transition: When you leave the back-through, lope on the right lead directly to the marker to dismount and mount.

- The pattern usually states whether you go on the right or left side of the marker. If the pattern calls for the horse's head to be at the cone, you put it there.

- When you walk to the cone and stop, square up your horse before you dismount. Don't make this a big issue, but when all four feet are fairly square, he's less apt to take a step when you get off or on him. When he's not square, your horse must take a step to stay balanced.

Teaching your horse to stand quietly and wait for you to move him is key to a smooth mount.

- After you stop and square your horse, give him just a second before you dismount. If you immediately step off, you catch him off-guard. Shift your weight slightly in your saddle to let him know you're dismounting so he's prepared for it. Do that weight-shift at home every time you dismount, and your horse knows what to expect.

- Dismount with your left hand on your horse's neck. That lets your horse know you need to balance yourself before you step off him. Your right hand is on the saddle horn.

- Most people leave the foot deep in the stirrup when they dismount. It's best to have your boot about halfway out of the stirrup. Something could spook your horse, and your foot could hang in the stirrup. That's a good habit, especially if you ride colts, so your foot comes out of the stirrup easily.

- When you remount your horse, have your reins straight and even. Practice that at home. Some people even mark their reins to be sure they're even. If your reins aren't, it's no big deal. Simply fix them before you move your horse.

- If you throw the left rein over your horse's neck before you mount him, a judge could call that a disqualification. You ride one-handed, so the ends of both reins should be on the same side as your rein hand.

- With your reins in your left hand on your horse's neck, put your foot in the stirrup, grab the horn with your right hand, and get on like you mean it. Don't be tentative about mounting your horse.

- Using the horn is sometimes hard to do, but don't grab the cantle of your saddle, or the skirts. If you must do that, use the mounting block that's usually in the arena and legal to use.

- If you step on your horse and ride forward immediately, before long, your horse just waits to feel a butt hit the saddle before he leaves. Make a point of standing still a minute. Your horse shouldn't move until you cue him, and it's good for him to know that.

- It's easy to work at home with a horse that's been allowed to move immediately. All you have to do is sit there and wait until your horse is through dancing around and stands still before you move. Do that consistently, and he learns to wait for you to tell him to go forward.

- Making an antsy horse stand is such a simple thing, but can become a big issue. A rider gets halfway on and the horse steps forward, which throws the rider off-balance. Then his leg flops on the horse's butt, which scares the horse, so he jumps, and the rider hits the ground. If you drive your foot deep into the stirrup, your foot can hang there just long enough for your horse to jerk you down—and then he could kick you right in the face or step on you. Teach your horse to stand while you mount and dismount so he learns to wait for you.

- Although no penalty is assessed when your horse shifts his weight to balance as you mount or dismount, you can be penalized 1 to 5 points, depending on the number of steps your horse takes, when he should be standing still.

Trail Showmanship

- The important thing is to know your trail pattern. Go through it in your mind, and how you need to cue your horse for each maneuver. You must really be on your toes for your horse to perform at specific points in the arena.

- Faster isn't better in the versatility trail class. Go through the pattern at a moderate speed, but smoothly. Be thoughtful and meticulous in what you do. That's what a trail performance should be.

- A good versatility trail score all comes down to showing your horse's ability to go through the maneuvers and obstacles and remain quiet and very responsive.

- Don't go so fast that your horse can't handle the pressure. If he gets antsy or on the muscle, you're in trouble. Even if he doesn't misbehave much, a judge can see the difference.

- Transitions with your horse are virtually what the versatility trail class is all about. It's kind of like the ranch riding, but in the trail class you do transitions with obstacles to show how quiet and relaxed your horse can be around anything.

Obstacle Acceptance

A solid, seasoned horse has seen a variety of obstacles and has been given time to learn he has nothing to fear. Working on any type trail obstacle helps get a horse broke. When you approach a new obstacle, think about what's worked in the past.

For example, your horse might have to walk by or over a tarp in the versatility, and tarps are used for blinders on the fences in the cutting pen. If tarps bother your horse, think about the approach to the bridge obstacle and take a similar approach with the tarp until it becomes part of the background scenery. You also might fasten a tarp down in your horse's pen and put his feed trough on top of it, or tie a tarp to your horse's fence until he becomes accustomed to it.

- Whatever you do when you introduce your horse to anything new, you must use good judgment. If you aren't sure what to do in a situation, ask a knowledgeable person to help you.

- Any time you introduce your horse to a new obstacle or experience, pick the place to do it. Be sure your horse can't hurt himself on anything in the area where you work and that your pen can hold him.

- If you don't have the time to really address a particular issue on a given day, usually it's best not to address it at all right then. You don't want to be forced into turning out your horse when he still thinks an obstacle is bad or scary. It takes time to do things right, and if you mess up, the next time it's twice as hard to get your horse over the problem.

- Walk back and forth and around a "spook" but keep your horse busy thinking about something else. Sometimes riding right past something scary does more good than you think because your horse realizes the spook doesn't bother you.

- When you try to ride up to a spook and get uptight or mad because your horse won't go there, he thinks the spook has spooked you, too. That makes things worse. Your horse feeds off you like he would another horse, and misunderstands the situation.

- Don't anticipate a problem with your horse. If he spooks at something the first time, don't expect him to do that every time. Otherwise, your horse feeds off your anxiety.

- At a show, when you see horses spook from an obstacle, don't sit there and let your horse watch that repeatedly. Before long, your horse "knows" a monster is there. Horses are smart, and body language is one of their ways to communicate, so turn your horse's butt to the problem and don't let him watch other horses spook at an obstacle.

Build the correct muscle memory you need for roping horseback.

13

LEARN THE ROPES

Roping cattle, along with reining and cow work, make up the working ranch-horse portion of the versatility event. This chapter focuses on basic rope-handling, and cattle-handling basics and cutting are covered in the following chapters. Combining the reining maneuvers you already know into a complete pattern for working ranch-horse competition is discussed in the final chapter.

In the roping part of the ranch-horse competition, a versatility contestant is allowed two throws to rope and stop a cow with a legal catch. In an American Quarter Horse Association versatility class, the rider cannot tie his rope to the saddle horn, but must dally it around the horn. Some associations allow a contestant to tie his rope on the horn. But either way, the judge scores the horse's ability to track, rate and stop the cow in the arena.

Fortunately, I'm a rancher and have been all my life, so this part of the versatility class is easier for me than it is for some people. But I still must pay attention when I rope to be sure that my horse and I don't get into trouble. I can't emphasize enough how important it is to develop safe rope-handling skills. You can get hurt.

Entire books and videos cover this one aspect of versatility ranch-horse competition. Anybody who ropes needs solid information from the start so he can keep himself and his horse safe. Playing things safe can be something as simple as using a roping glove to protect a hand or as important as dallying with a thumb up to keep from losing it. For backup, a ranch cowboy always carries a knife; he might need it. Anybody who ropes should carry one, too.

What follows only scratches the surface about roping. This includes a few things I've learned through the years that might help somebody avoid common mistakes people often make at my clinics.

Develop and practice correct muscle memory when learning to rope so you can be competitive and stay safe.

The Performance Goal

The goal here is to become comfortable handling a rope before you rope live cattle. Besides building the skills you need for the working ranch-horse class, you also prepare yourself and your horse for the dummy-roping obstacle in the versatility trail class.

Afoot or horseback, when you practice roping a dummy, you build the muscle memory to handle your rope in a competitive situation. When you're horseback behind a live cow, there's a lot to think about in addition to building and delivering your loop. The more you practice those basics at home, then the less you have to consciously think about them in the show arena.

Even if you don't think of yourself as a roper and don't plan ever to back into the roping box at a jackpot, think of yourself as a horseman building a great horse you'd really like to ride. Think of roping a dummy and eventually live cattle as more opportunities to use the training you've put on your horse so far. Then you really build confidence between you and a versatile horse—yours.

Review Your Skills

You develop a totally new skill set when you first learn to handle a rope. Although you might not have any roping skills to review right now, you can develop some soon. As you add to your understanding, you realize that roping is a lot like horse training—success often comes right back to basic skills that are the foundation to a smooth run. As you progress with your roping, the skills in this chapter become the ones you review in the future to stay smooth in your work.

When it's time to get horseback and rope the dummy, warm up your horse first by going over the basic flexion, collection, softness and body control exercises you've been doing. Then your horse is tuned and ready to give you a good response at the dummy.

Coil Your Rope

As I mentioned in the equipment chapter, I suggest using a poly rope, rather than nylon, for learning how to rope and for roping muleys, cattle without horns, in the versatility ranch-horse competition. A poly rope is a

Roll your right wrist to make a coil in your rope and be sure to lay the coils smoothly into your left hand.

little more forgiving than a nylon. When you deliver a loop with a poly rope, it pretty much just stays where you put it, but a nylon rope can bounce. If you don't have much control of a rope yet, you can have trouble managing the nylon. The poly rope is easiest to use when you're learning, and you always can switch later.

- Most people rope right-handed, so that's the approach here although now there also are left-spin ropes on the market for left-handed people. If you're left-handed, do basically the opposite of what's described here. It's also good to talk with a left-handed roper for hands-on information.

- To coil your rope, hold the tail of it in your left hand with the end coming from the bottom of your hand to hang down almost to your left foot. Any longer than that, and the tail can get in your way when you're horseback.

- With your right hand, grasp the rope underhanded in front of your left hand and slide your right hand down the rope to about arm's length. Then roll your right hand up and over, bringing it toward your left hand to make the first coil.

- Put your first coil in your left hand and continue to coil your entire rope, moving each coil to your left hand. How the coils lay in your hand is important. As you make each coil, lay it smoothly into your left hand so you can drop your coils easily if that's necessary. If your coils are in a wad and you get into a wreck, you can't let go of the coils as easily. That's not safe.

- If the rope kinks, or twists, as you make a coil, take out the kink before you continue building your coils. If necessary, twist your hand the other direction as you make the coil to get rid of any kinks. After you've coiled your rope a few times, you develop a feel for it and soon know, without looking, when there's a kink in your rope.

From your right hand to your shirt buttons is a good starting place for measuring the length of the bridge in your rope.

Build A Bridge

When you use your right hand to pick up a coil from your left hand and build a loop, you create a "bridge" in your rope that runs between your coils in your left hand and the loop in your right.

- There isn't an exact measurement for the length of your bridge. After you build a loop, hold your coils, the left side of your bridge, about where your shirt buttons are. Then extend your right hand to the side. That's a good place to start. As you learn and practice roping, you can adjust the length of your bridge to whatever is comfortable for you.

- When you rope muleys, the bridge typically is a little bit wider than the bridge you might use when roping horned cattle. With horned cattle, a smaller bridge helps you rope a little faster and helps create the curl you need to catch the horns. Since you rope necks on muley cattle in versatility competition, you don't need quite as much speed, and that little slower loop can come down and around to catch your cow.

Build Your Loop

The eye in your rope is the honda. The tail of your rope runs through the honda to form the loop and the area from the honda to your right hand, made of those two pieces of rope, is called the spoke. The loop itself is one strand of rope, and the slack that comes through the honda and goes to your coils is the second.

- To build a loop, hold the coils in your left hand and use your right to pick up the first coil. You must now feed the rope through the honda in that first coil to make a large loop, and there are several ways to do that.

- For beginners, an easy way to feed the loop is to hold the eye of the honda and slide it toward you, then around the rope

Here's a general idea of how long the spoke should be. Choking down on a short spoke really can interfere with your swing.

toward the next coil in your left hand. Feed the rope around and through the honda until you have the size loop you want to use.

- You also can roll that first small loop over the top of your right hand to feed more rope into the loop without the rope kinking as you make the loop larger. That looks cool, and that's how most people do it, but until you're familiar with a rope, you might have a hard time doing that, especially when you're horseback.

- Don't put the slack, the strand of rope coming through the honda to make the bridge to your coils, inside the loop in your right hand. When you do, your rope really twists. That strand of rope needs to be on the outside of your loop. Such a little thing might not seem to matter much, but is a big issue. Where the strand lays can make the swing of your rope so different. If your rope twists badly in your hands, put that strand to the outside of your loop, and things should improve.

- Once you've built your loop, allow plenty of distance for the spoke between your right hand and the honda. If you choke down short on the spoke, that really affects your swing and your roping, and not in a good way.

You can roll the loop over your right hand to feed it, or enlarge the loop.

- As for the size of the loop, it's better to have enough loop, rather than too little, so bigger is better. With a large loop, you can build more momentum into your swing to help carry and deliver the loop. With a small loop, you must swing really hard to do that. Start by using a loop that runs from the ground to about shoulder-high, and then adjust the size of your loop from there.

Take a Swing

The more you practice a correct swing when you rope the dummy, the more correct your delivery can be when you throw your rope. You also build the correct muscle memory you need to rope at a show when your mind might be on other things.

- With the loop in your right hand, bring your hand up and forward to swing your loop from right to left in front of you. Then, as your loop rotates from left to right behind you, your wrist also rotates, and your palm turns up.

- Practice swinging a big loop. With a little loop, most people typically don't bring up the elbow enough as they swing to keep a loop open. A big loop forces you to use your entire arm and shoulder and raise your elbow. As you swing, your wrist also helps carry your arm through the rotation, and that helps you swing correctly, too. Mainly your elbow and wrist keep your loop open.

- When you swing, all the power is in your shoulder. If you don't use your shoulder, you don't have any power or distance when you deliver, or throw, your loop. Use your whole shoulder in the swing to develop the muscle memory you need.

- Don't take a death grip on your rope as you swing it. Then your loop figure-eights instead of staying open. Grip your rope loosely so it can move in your hand.

- As you practice swinging, first work at a medium speed. Later you can learn to change the speed of your swing and how to speed up or slow down your rope.

- Obviously, when a cow gains speed, you must swing harder to get your rope to

When you swing a rope, all the power to deliver the loop is in your shoulder.

the cow, but you never change your basic form in the swing. If you do, you miss the cow. Once you learn basic roping maneuvers correctly, the only thing that changes is your speed, the same as it does when your horse learns a new maneuver.

- No matter if you swing fast or slow, and there are times when you must slow down things, keep your elbow up and the form of your swing the same. Otherwise, you have what's called a soft loop. Soft-looping usually happens when a roper "weenie-arms" in his swing. He drops his elbow and loses his power, and that slows down everything.

- The typical mistake in swinging a rope happens when somebody swings with only his elbow and the wrist. He doesn't use his whole shoulder to build power and momentum into the swing. When he throws the rope, it's just out there, but without any real power to send the loop where it needs to go.

Deliver Your Loop

Roping is all muscle memory. The more you practice and the more you deliver a loop, the better you get at catching cattle. Improving your roping is that simple.

- When you deliver your loop, look where you want your rope to go. If you see only the top of the calf's head, that's what you rope. Then you topknot the cow, and your rope comes off.

- To rope muley cattle, look about where the cow's shoulders and head join. That puts the bottom of your loop where it should be when you deliver it. As you swing, your hand rolls over and you can point your index finger toward that spot. Then you have the dip, or downward motion, in your rope you need to get it around the cow's neck.

- The bottom part of your loop is what you can control in the delivery. Every time you put that part of your loop right where you want it on the cow, the rest of the loop gets everything else into your rope and you catch.

- No matter what you rope, the bottom part of your hand controls your loop,

In the delivery, look where you want your loop to go. You can even point your index finger to target the spot as you release your loop.

the bottom part of it. When you practice, act like you're going to slap that spot on the roping dummy with the middle and bottom of your hand.

- When you throw your loop on a muley, usually you drop one coil from your left hand. Unlike a horned steer, a muley's face usually is down, so you must have more rope down in front of the cow. The weight of your rope going down helps pull that coil out of your hand. With horned cattle, you seldom drop a coil so you can use that short bridge to help bring your rope around the horns.

Afoot at the Dummy

No matter your position at the dummy, always swing your loop with good form, and use your arm and shoulder to keep the loop at the same angle in relation to the cow. Always look where you want your loop to go and remember to control the bottom of your loop to get it there. Then you build correct muscle memory.

- When you're afoot and rope the dummy, don't get too far back at first. Stand 5 or 6 feet back and off the dummy's left hip. That's not too far from where you'd be on your horse.

- Rope the dummy from that initial position until you're totally comfortable using your rope. Then change to rope from different positions. The more you do, the better you learn to handle your rope and deliver your loop.

- Think about roping like a rancher does. My goal as a rancher is to rope and catch 100 percent of the time. The less I have to run my cattle to rope them, the better off my cattle are. That approach works pretty good for me in the versatility class, too. It also can work for you at the practice dummy.

- Remember: Not everything is the same every time you go into the pen to rope cattle. You must be able to adjust to fit any situation. The more you practice, the more the basics of roping become second nature to you, and the better you can adjust when things change.

Handling Slack Afoot

You might think that how you handle your slack when you're afoot at the dummy isn't a big deal, but it can be. You start to develop habits at the dummy that can help you become a really good roper or habits that can get in the way of that and hurt your versatility score.

- If you rope with a lot of dip in your loop, you might naturally want to handle your slack like a calf-roper, but grab your slack with your thumb up and bring it all the way back to your hip. You don't go to your horn with your rope until the cow pulls your hand forward and even with the saddle horn. Then you let the rope slip in your hand and slide the rope around the horn. Practice handling your slack now for when you go to the horn later.

- Build the same muscle memory afoot that you need when you're horseback.

Handle your slack at the dummy correctly from the start so you don't have to break any bad habits later.

A Rope-Broke Horse

If you're new to versatility ranch-horse and have never roped before, maybe you found that solid horse with cattle experience described in the earlier chapter, the horse that can help you learn about handling cattle and roping. Then swinging a rope or dragging one behind your horse isn't a problem.

If you aren't sure if your horse is rope-broke, use common sense, a little caution and good judgment when you approach him with a rope. Always carry a knife; you might need it to stay out of a wreck.

If you don't have a clue what a rope-broke horse is, ask a top roper in your area for help, or go to a roping clinic so you can learn solid information and good skills from the start.

An entire book could be written about rope-breaking horses and teaching them to pull something at the end of a rope. This is just a quick description of how I first approach any horse with my lariat rope. A young horse obviously doesn't know much about a rope, but sometimes a mature horse doesn't have any rope experience at all. Either way, my approach is the same.

- I don't test a fresh horse to see if he's rope-broke. I wait until the end of a normal work session before I approach him with the rope.

- Sometimes I first use a coiled rope to "sack out" a horse. I rub the rope all over the horse until he's comfortable with the feel and sound of the rope. I might throw the tail of the rope over my horse's back and let it touch his feet and legs. The big mistake people make is using a new rope that sounds like a rattlesnake to a horse. An old rope, lead rope or longe line is better for this.

- Usually I tie a horse safely in the pen before I walk around swinging my rope. If that doesn't bother the horse, I move to the next step. If it does, I keep swinging until he's okay with that.

- Then I move close to the horse and put my left hand with the coils on the swell of my saddle and swing my rope on the right. That puts me between the horse and the loop, kind of a security blanket for the horse. If the horse moves, I can use my left hand on the saddle to push myself away from him.

- Next, I take the horse into a small pen and get on him. Before I build a loop to swing, I shorten my left rein a little bit. Then with my coils and rein in my left hand, I ride my horse in a left-hand circle and swing the loop with my right hand. With the shortened left rein, I can take hold of a horse, if it's necessary, to disengage his hip—and never quit swinging my loop. I ride and swing until the horse accepts the situation.

- Most horses accept a rope fairly quickly, but sometimes a horse simply has to realize that he must deal with it since I use a rope almost daily in my ranch work, just like I do that horse. The more matter-of-fact I am about the rope, usually the quicker and more accepting the horse becomes.

- I can't stress enough how important it is to use good judgment anytime a horse and a rope are involved. Something might go wrong, and the horse, the rider or both can get hung in the rope. That's why good cowboys carry knives.

Horseback at the Dummy

When you're really comfortable afoot and roping the dummy, saddle up and rope the dummy from your horse. At least warm up your horse before you start roping the dummy, but it's best to wait until your entire ride for the day is done. Then your horse is really relaxed.

- When you ride with split reins in your left hand and have a finger between them, carry your rope coils on top of your reins.

- A timed-event roper brings his roping rein from the bottom of his hand up and over the top of his fist, but usually splits the rein with his little finger.

- With a romal, your reins also come from the bottom of your hand over the top, but you can't split the rein with your little finger in the ranch-horse versatility classes. That's not legal.

- When riding left-handed with a romal in the versatility, you usually put the romal tail on the right side of your horse. But when you rope right-handed and use a

When roping, the tail of the romal falls on the left side of the horse so the tail doesn't interfere with your roping.

Here's how to carry your coils and split reins in your left hand.

romal, put the romal tail to the left side so that it's out of your way.

- When you're horseback to rope the dummy, initially position your horse's jaw so that it clears the dummy or bale of hay. As you practice, adjust to find the ideal position that suits you and your horse and then move around from there.

- Start roping the dummy when you're horseback the same way you did afoot. Stand your horse in that ideal position and practice there until you can handle your rope and catch consistently. Then start moving around the dummy and roping from different places.

Handling the Slack Horseback

Roping the dummy when you're horseback helps you start building the correct muscle memory you need to handle your slack when you rope a cow in the ranch-horse class. You then automatically do the right things whenever you compete.

- When you're horseback and catch that dummy, come back to your hip with the slack like you did when you were afoot. Hold the rope out from your hip and alongside your horse, but don't be in a hurry to go to the horn and practice dallying. If you hurry right there when you're behind a cow, your horse could step over the rope.

- Even though the dummy and your horse don't move, think about what happens in the arena when a real calf and your horse are moving. As your horse rates his speed and the calf continues ahead, your hand moves from your hip to come even with the saddle horn. That's when you let the rope slide in your hand and slide it around the horn. Don't just grab the rope and hang on; you have to let it slide around the horn.

- The main thing to remember: Let the cow and the horse take the slack out of your rope before you go to your horn. Use the opportunity at the dummy to

Practice horseback at the roping dummy just as if you had a live cow on the end of your rope.

build your awareness of what you must do with your slack so you're prepared for the real thing in the arena.

- Keep this in mind while you prepare yourself for arena roping. In versatility competition, as you hold your slack to let your horse and cow take care of it, keep riding your horse. A lot of people don't. When they realize they've roped something, they get nervous or scared, and quit riding altogether. Keep riding your horse until you've dallied the rope.

Dally Your Rope

There's no time it's more important to build the correct muscle memory than when you take your dallies on the horn. One thoughtless moment here and you can lose a thumb. It's so important to learn how to handle your rope safely.

- When you first hook your rope counterclockwise around the front of your horn, don't take a death grip on the rope. You can't take your dallies if you

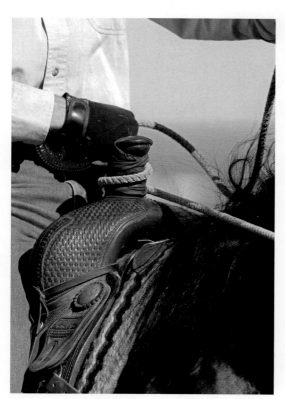

Dally your rope safely. You can lose a thumb with a moment's carelessness.

do. Let the rope slide through your hand as you wrap your rope on your horn. Don't take hold and pinch the rope until you're ready to stop your cow.

- Important: Keep your right thumb up and away from the rope as you take your dallies counterclockwise around the horn. Be smart and keep your thumb.

- Even though it's hard to practice dallying without looking down at your horn—don't. When you look at your horn, you can get in a wreck, and nobody wants to lose a thumb.

- Tying the rope onto the horn isn't allowed in American Quarter Horse Association versatility classes. But, for example, in Ranch Horse Association of America events, that's optional; you can tie on or dally. When you show in a versatility class, check the rules.

Practice Dallying

Here's the best way to practice taking your dallies correctly and probably the most beneficial thing you can do when it comes to dallying a rope. All you need is your horse, your rope and a partner afoot to hold the end of your rope.

- Put on your roping glove and get on your horse. Throw the loop end of your rope to a partner standing on the ground in front of you and hold the coils and tail with your left hand. Have your slack in your right hand back at your hip.

- Ask your partner to walk forward carrying the rope. The person shouldn't look back at you because he or she might subconsciously make adjustments to take care of you. Then you don't learn what you need to know about dallying.

- As your partner walks forward and the rope comes taut, your right hand comes forward to your horn. As it does, let your rope slide in your hand and slide it around the horn. Be sure to look ahead, not down at your horn, as you take your wraps, and keep your thumb up so it doesn't get caught in a dally.

- With your partner instead of a 600-pound steer on the end of your rope, there's no big jerk. Everything moves slowly, so you safely can build the correct muscle memory you need for versatility competition. Plus, you can practice dallying as long as your partner is willing to keep walking.

- You also can use this same method to learn to let your rope slide around your horn and give slack to a cow. Don't grip your rope tightly in you right hand, but let it slide through your hand to give slack as your partner walks forward. Then make the correct moves and dally your rope around your horn again.

The best way to practice dallying safely and correctly requires a partner who's willing to work afoot.

An Ambidextrous Roper

Most every tack store carries left-handed ropes now, and you can find anything on the Internet, but that wasn't always the case. In the past, a left-handed roper sometimes set up a right-handed rope so that it was completely backward. Even though he could rope with it, he really had to pay attention, especially when he dallied, because the rope could get a big furl in it.

Although my dad is a left-handed roper, I learned to rope right-handed. When I was a kid, I broke my leg and couldn't do much. But I could rope, and I did—until I got really tired. That's when I taught myself to rope left-handed, too.

No, the photo isn't flopped. I can rope left-handed, too.

Two minds, yours and your horse's, must communicate to the third, the cow's, that you have the advantage in position.

14
CATTLE-HANDLING BASICS

Reading cattle is a big hole in many people's versatility programs, simply because they haven't had the opportunity to work cattle. Learning about cattle is a big draw at my clinics, and most people are enthusiastic and want to become accomplished at handling cattle. Being a cowboy still intrigues people, and cattle are such a big part of that.

The challenges that a cowboy experiences make versatility competition unique. One challenge is learning how to maneuver a horse well into any position to control the cow. Another challenge is reading the cow to know what position the horse should take.

Working cattle involves three minds. Two of those minds, yours and your horse's, must communicate completely to convey to the third—the cow you don't have under control—that you have the advantage in position. Good cow work is getting into that position fast enough to control your cow.

The Performance Goal

When you learn to read a cow, you really understand where the "right" spot is—the one that makes a cow move in a certain way. You also realize how much difference 6 inches, forward or back of that spot, can make. Those few inches can determine

Learning about cattle—how to read them and maneuver them with a horse—draws many people to ranch-horse competition.

whether you get the cow to do what you want, and that affects your versatility score.

Versatility competition requires several types of cow work. You must cut a cow from the herd, box the cow at one end of an arena, turn it back in each direction along the fence line, and then rope the cow. Everything comes down to reading the cow, just like it does if you go to a practice roping or to help your neighbor gather his cattle.

Review Your Skills

Anytime you have a problem with your horse not being as light and responsive as you'd like, or with your roping, go back to the basics. When you do, you soon figure out where the problem lies. That's why flexing and suppling your horse in the warm-up, just like your roping practice at the dummy, is important. You figure out when you have a little problem before it becomes a big one. Plus, going over the basics really helps you and your horse develop the correct muscle memory you need to perform well. The list at the end of the book gives you a framework for building the basic skills you need.

Learn to Read

Reading a cow means understanding what that cow thinks before the cow acts on its thinking. Your horse's position is what you use to counteract the cow's thinking. That's what cattle-handling is—being in that specific place to counteract what the cow is about to do. It's almost like playing chess.

It takes practice to learn to think like a cow thinks. The cow wants to go back to its buddies. The question is how willing that cow is to test you. When you have an idea about that, you can put your horse in the correct position and help him learn to read cattle.

- The best way to learn to read a cow is to put only one in the pen and move it around with your horse. If you haven't worked cattle before, don't start with three or four cows. Then you must deal with them, plus try to teach yourself position and work with your horse, too.

- Ride your horse slowly and quietly behind that one cow. Watch the cow's reaction to you being close behind it or farther away. Then ride to another position on the cow, maybe to the side, and see what happens. Evaluate how the cow responds to your horse's position.

- Dealing with cattle is fairly basic. You begin to figure out how much pressure it takes in a certain place on the cow to move the cow forward. You learn that when you ride to another spot, the cow might stop. You find out where to be to get the cow to turn and face you.

- Each cow has a safety zone. When you crowd that cow's safety zone, the cow leaves. The safety zone on some cattle is small, but on others is far away from that cow, and you must recognize that.

- Pay attention to an individual cow's safety zone. Where you are in relation to that safety zone affects what that particular cow does, whether it stays or goes. As you move the practice cow, you learn the effect pressure from different positions has on the cow's safety zone.

- The closer you get to a cow and its safety zone, the more advantage you give the cow. But you can control a flighty cow with a large safety zone the same way you control a soft-minded cow with a small zone. You just have to be quicker than the flighty cow to hold or stop it.

- When a flighty practice cow runs across the pen to get away, you soon figure out how to ride along the fence and drive the cow around the pen to control the situation. You also might learn that when you put too much pressure on a flighty cow, it can run into the fence.

- When your horse is in position on a cow, he doesn't have to move a great distance to make the cow move forward or back, or stop. Actually the range of maneuverability comes down to about 6 inches. If you're 6 inches behind the position where you need to be, a cow tries you. If you and your horse are about even with the cow, whether or not the cow tries you is a question of how much stamina it has. If you're 6 inches ahead in position, you can stop that cow. Your horse's position on a cow makes all the difference in what the cow does.

- Getting a cow to turn its face toward you is known as drawing a cow, and you do that when you must turn one. When you catch the cow's right eye, for instance,

A quiet, calm approach is best whether you're dealing with one cow or several.

and then slow down and drop back and away from the cow, you draw the cow toward your horse. If that cow ever stops and looks at you, you can use the draw to set up your working situation. Drawing a cow to you isn't always easy, especially when you want to stop the cow instead of turn it.

• Whenever you can, watch someone who knows how to handle cattle work a cow and ask him to explain what he's doing. When you can see what happens between the horse and cow, and also understand why, you really grasp the knowledge.

Beyond the Fear

That 6-inch range of maneuverability, described earlier, is why it's important that your horse learn how to read a cow, too. No matter how responsive a horse is, if he must wait for someone to tell him what to do, he's too late on a cow. You simply can't signal your horse quickly enough to put him in the right position to stop a cow, hold one or turn one back. It takes too long for the signal from your hands to get to your horse.

But you can help your horse learn to read cattle in the practice pen, where you can slow down and give him time to understand cattle. When you can help him learn to take position on a cow, your horse can learn to read cattle. When he can read cattle, he can control them.

• A horse that's scared of the cow at first usually makes one of the best cow horses. If you introduce him to cattle slow and easy the first time, you probably never have another issue with his fear.

183

as usual, and go through your normal warm-up with the cow in the pen.

- After the edge is off your horse, occasionally lope by the cow closely enough that the cow moves. When the cow moves, keep your horse moving. Don't try to do anything with the cow at this point. If your horse gets scared, don't make a big issue of it. Keep working him gradually toward the cow until the cow becomes part of the woodwork. Before long, you can drop your horse in behind the cow and go to work.

- If you aren't very experienced with cattle and introduce your horse to a cow, your horse feeds off your nervousness. He knows something is different about you with the cow in the pen. Your horse thinks you're scared of the cow, so figures he ought to be scared of the cow, too. Keep riding anyway. As the edge comes off, you get a little more confident. Your horse feels that, too, and decides there's no reason to be scared.

Track One Cow

Now teach your horse to track one cow in the pen. It's another way for your horse to get comfortable around cattle, and you also must track cattle when you rope in the versatility. When you teach your horse to track, he learns to go to a certain position and stay there, hooked up with the cow, so that you can rope.

- People go wrong in tracking because they don't really know where to look at the cow—his butt, his shoulder, his back, or whatever. When you track a cow, look at the head and the cow's eye.

- The head moves the cow, and the eye moves the head, so watch the eye. Your position in relation to the cow's eye creates the cow's movement and affects where the cow goes. The pressure you put on the cow from your position is pressure you actually put on that cow's eye.

- When you're behind a cow, it still watches you out of one eye or the other, like a horse does when you walk behind him. You can control the cow because

For a horse to learn to read cattle, you must give him time to figure out how his position on a cow affects the cow.

- If your horse is scared of cattle, don't cram a cow down his throat. Your horse only gets more scared, and it takes even longer for him to become comfortable around cattle.

- Introduce your horse to cattle by putting one cow in the pen and then riding in the pen. Be passive about your horse's fear. Ignore the cow, so your horse is okay with ignoring it. Ride your horse

When you track a cow, watch the cow's eye. Your position in relation to the cow's eye affects its movement and direction.

you can move to its right side and bring the cow right, or vice versa. You learn to draw a cow to you, as well as push one away from you.

- When you track a cow, always maintain control of your horse. Some people run a cow, but have no stop or turn on their horses, and that gets them into trouble. When you have control and practice tracking, you can maneuver your horse wherever you want, slow down things and give him a chance to learn.

- You don't have to track a cow fast to teach your horse. It's best to start tracking the cow in a trot. If the cow tries to run, put a little more distance between your horse

and the cow. That takes pressure off the cow and brings it back to a trot.

- Trot around the pen behind the cow, then move by the cow. When the cow stops, stop your horse and back him three or four steps. Use your feet to make him stay off the bridle. Then go with the cow again and do the same thing, and do that on both sides. That's how you start training your horse to "cow up."

- If the cow you track turns to go the other way, let your horse come across to the side and keep tracking. Here's where your warm-up exercises pay off in his quick, easy response in the turn. He can gather up and work off his back end.

- Learn how much pressure it takes—how close you have to be to the cow—to move the cow forward and how far back you must be to take off pressure and stop the cow. As a cow tires, that amount of pressure, or distance, can change considerably.

- If you're too close, a cow usually lets you chase it around the pen. But if you back off the cow a little, and then trot up, the cow usually stops and probably turns to go the other way. So do those things and learn how your horse's position affects the cow you track.

- When you track or drive a cow, you might think you must be behind the cow all the time. However, you can drive a cow from its side, too. Drive your practice cow around the pen from behind at first. Then find out about working on the side, up near the shoulders, where you can adjust your position to make the cow go forward or turn it back.

- Where you go within that 6 inches of maneuverability can determine whether you turn a cow or move it forward. Step ahead to the front of those 6 inches to turn the cow. Drop toward the end of those 6 inches, and you drive the cow forward, especially if you're at the side and have the cow between you and a fence. However, when you do that in the middle of a pasture, a cow usually travels straight away from you unless the herd is pulling the cow like a magnet.

- As your practice cow changes speed, your horse must handle the transitions in speed to handle the cow. That helps your horse learn to deal with anything, so nothing catches him off-guard.

- Although you don't circle a cow in the versatility ranch-horse competition, circling a cow is a really good thing to do because you and your horse can learn so much about position. Drive your practice cow in a tight circle in each direction. You don't have to do that fast, and you might lose the cow a time or two, but you also learn about where to be to take control the cow.

- Tracking a cow, even roping it, also is one of the best things to do with an older horse that's a little sour about going down the fence in the versatility ranch-horse class. Tracking and roping gets a horse's mind off stopping and turning the cow back on the fence.

The Dry Work

When your horse is ready to work a cow, first review the cutter-type rollback. When you can back your horse into the circle and then turn into the rollback, he knows how to keep his butt underneath him, and he has the muscle memory to come back easily through the turn when you actually put him on a cow. When a horse knows only the forward-type rollback and turns with a cow, the cow has the advantage and can get by the horse.

- Use dry work to prepare your horse to work cattle. Ride him across the pen in a straight line, stop, back, pull his nose through the turn and let him go straight across to the other side. With repetitive turns, your horse learns what to do without picking up bad habits he might develop while working cattle when he's unprepared to make the correct moves. Trot, stop, back and turn your horse until he's totally comfortable and responsive.

- Without the dry work, when your horse is first put on a cow, the horse thinks about what you're doing to back him here and send him there; he's not thinking about the cow. The dry work helps to pattern your horse so that when he's in front of the cow, everything comes quickly and correctly.

- A lot goes through your horse's mind when you put him on a cow. Working the cow might be new to your horse, but he's not hot or bothered at first because he understands what to do. You've already shown him the moves to make in the dry work, so he can focus on the cow.

- When do you put your horse on a cow, and your horse already knows how to come through the turn, he picks up on what the cow does much faster.

The dry work, stopping and backing into a cutter-type rollback, prepares your horse to make the same moves when he first learns to stop and turn with a slow cow.

Work One Cow

You and your horse should be ready to work a cow now. The main thing to understand is that working cattle in the practice pen, especially at first, isn't a timed event. Go slow so your horse can develop the skills he needs. You change things when you work a cow instead of tracking it, so give your horse time to get comfortable with the change. Working cattle is like anything else—the slower you go, the more correct the muscle memory you build. Once that muscle memory is a subconscious thing, the quickness comes.

As your horse develops the correct muscle memory, the speed comes and he learns to stop and turn with fast cattle.

- After your horse is comfortable with cattle, ride your horse into the stop position on a cow. With your leg about where the cow's shoulder meets the rib cage, stop the cow. The minute the cow stops, stop your horse.

- When you stop the cow and the cow turns, at first don't let your horse turn with the cow. Instead, back your horse a few steps and pull his nose through the turn, the same way you do in the dry work, so he understands what you want.

After turning with a cow, ride right back into the stop position on the cow. Be aware of the difference 6 inches in your position can make on the cow.

Work Anything

You don't have to work an actual cow to give your horse experience. Work anything you can. Put it in the pen, the same as you do a cow, and then move it around with your horse. Learn to position your horse to control the animal so you can do what you want to do.

Some people work buffalo, but you must have a strong facility for that. Buffalo can be tough on green horses, but do tend to last longer than practice cattle and have a lot of stamina.

A burro is inexpensive and easy to keep, but soon quits working for you. Some people use goats. They quickly get smart about what you're doing, but they're also inexpensive and usually are easy to find. I've even seen people using their children to work horses, and I've worked my horses on the peacocks at my barn. Even two horses and riders can work one another, with one horse and rider being the cow, and the other horse and rider the cutter.

When practice cattle aren't available, Holly and I use a "walk-cow" to sharpen a horse's response. See Chapter 15 for more on the walk-cow.

- When you pull your horse's nose through the turn, he can't drop his shoulder. If his shoulder drops, he can't make a clean turn and loses his draw-backward motion. Then the cow is way ahead of your horse.

- After your horse turns, catch up with the cow and ride into the stop position again. Stop the cow with your horse parallel to the cow. Then back your horse and pull

him through the turn and catch the cow again. Do this until your horse trots right to the cow and stops consistently. You'll be surprised at how quickly your horse wants to stop with the cow.

- Always work your cow in a straight line across the pen as you ride and stop. As you come across the pen, use your cow-side leg to help keep your horse's body soft. Stop, back and come across in the turn, right on that straight line. That sounds simple, but sometimes can be a tough thing to accomplish.

- When you ride two-handed and stop your horse, use a little more cow-side rein to pick up his shoulder and keep the cow-side of his rib cage soft. Then when you start backing, his body's shaped to come back easily with the cow.

- If you stop your horse but allow him to start the turn at the same time, your horse gets "front-endy." He doesn't work off his back end, and until he does, he never learns to make that pretty move turning back with the cow.

- When the cow turns, if your horse turns like he's going around a barrel, you're too late. The cow's gone, and that kills your cutting score. Go back to the dry work and teach your horse to use his back end and come around with his front end. Don't be in a hurry to go with the cow. Make sure your horse stops and draws, or backs, correctly before you bring his nose through the turn.

- Sometimes a horse stops and throws his hip to the side. When you stop and back your horse, he can't throw his hip because he must use it for the back and then the turn.

- Repetition and consistency are important with the stop, back and turn. Then your horse hooks onto a cow because it's easy. Your horse learns the correct move and makes it every time because he never knows anything different.

- Once your horse starts stopping on his own with a cow, don't forget to work on the stop, back and turn. You can't ingrain that enough in your horse. As he gets fluid in his stop, he learns the next move is to draw back, and then come through the turn, and he becomes fluid there, too. Always stop and back your horse through the turns.

- Later, when you go down the fence with a cow in the ranch-horse class, your horse's rib cage is soft, and he has that big stop and the prettiest comeback on a cow, all because he's learned to stop, back and turn. He's easy to ride then, too. But if you halfway stop and turn, your horse becomes hard to ride down the fence, really front-endy and rough.

- At some point before you compete in versatility cutting, you must ride your horse into a pen with a herd of cattle. When you do, focus on one cow, and your horse soon learns that the other cattle move to get out of his way. Spend a little time letting your horse get totally sure of that.

- As always, when your horse isn't responding well in the cattle work, go back to the basics.

*The cattle determine more world champions
than the cutters do.*

15
RANCH CUTTING

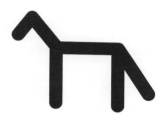

Some people watch ranch cutting competition and think a cow-savvy horse does all the work while others think the rider does. Neither way of thinking is totally accurate. A versatility cutting horse should be able to read cattle, and usually the cowier the horse, the better the score. The rider should be able to read cattle, too, to guide and direct his horse.

Granted, some horses naturally read cattle better than others, just as some people do, but when you can maneuver a soft, light horse into position on a cow, you and your horse can control that cow, and that's what cutting is all about.

The Performance Goal

In ranch cutting you have turn-back men and herd holders in the arena to help you, and your goal is to pull one cow out of the herd, hold it and show how well your horse can control the cow. For that to happen, you must develop your horse's

responsiveness, as well as work as many practice cattle as possible, so that you and your horse can do your job well. You also must learn to rely on your partners to help you achieve your goal. In those respects, versatility cutting competition isn't all that different from working cattle on the ranch.

Review Your Skills

You really enjoy the benefits from your warm-up exercises in the ranch cutting competition because your horse can be so soft and responsive when working a cow. Those correct responses are so ingrained in him, just like your direction is so subconscious and natural now, because the two of you have practiced the basics so often in your warm-up. Continue going over the basics to ensure that your horse maintains his level of performance. Following the last chapter is the list of basic skills you can incorporate in your warm-up routine.

In ranch cutting competition it all comes down to how much a rider trusts his horse.

Arena Helpers

In ranch cutting you have four helpers in the arena, all horseback—two turn-backs and two herd holders. The two turn-back riders have one important role—to make the cow move so that you can show the judge how well your horse works cattle. The two herd holders' jobs are just that—to hold the cattle in one area of the arena. The cattle know the herd holders are there, and that helps keep the cattle from running back and forth so much and getting in the way.

- Show management might supply the turn-back men and herd holders, or you can supply your own arena help.

- You also can be a herd holder or turn-back rider for another competitor. If that's the plan, take a spare horse to the event so you don't wear out your show horse. It also can desensitize him when you repeatedly push him at a cow and then pull him off a cow when turning back for someone else.

- When you select your turn-backs, try to find the two people you think understand cattle the most, the best cow hands at the competition. The turn-backs must read cattle well, so that they don't put too much pressure on you, to the point you can't hold your cow from the herd.

- The turn-back men also make a difference when you get your cow cut out of the herd, by making sure that you have enough room to work. When you work your cow, the herd holders help stop a herd from interfering with you, which helps you set your cow up in the middle of the pen and keep it there.

Two turn-back riders and two herd holders help each contestant in the cutting competition.

- Anytime you must keep a cow in the middle, the cow feels pressure and runs back and forth. The best thing the turn-backs can do then is back off, toward the outside of the pen, just enough to take pressure off the cow, so you can maintain control of it.

- Your herd holders usually can foresee when cattle might try to come out of the herd, on top of you and the cow you're working, and put those cattle back with the herd.

Cutting-Pen Cattle

In ranch cutting, the first cow you work is your designated, numbered cow. You then also select one additional, unnumbered cow to work within the 2-minute time limit. The advantage in versatility cutting is that nobody else can work your designated cow. At a National Cutting Horse Association event, for example, competitors who draw an early working position get the pick of the cattle.

- Regardless of how much riders settle the herd before the competition, cattle still can be a little flighty at first, but get more docile as the class progresses.

- A later working position in ranch cutting often is to your advantage. You usually can take your designated cow, which hasn't been cut, and make a better run because the whole herd has really settled.

- There's such variation on how fresh cutting cattle might work. If good cutters work the herd and hold the cattle, the cows learn that they can't get past a horse and soon quit trying to get back to the herd. Then the cattle don't really challenge a horse.

- If the cattle are fresh and the cutters are mediocre, they train the cattle to get past the horses. When a cow does that to a couple of horses, it can make things tough for you, even when you're in the right position on your cow.

When cutting cattle come from the same herd, chances are they have been handled in much the same way and have somewhat similar attitudes when they're worked.

- Although you can't do anything about the designated cow you draw in the versatility cutting, you pick the second cow you work. Watch the herd being settled and the other competitors work, so that you can select an unnumbered cow that might work to your advantage.

Bovine Breeds

Like some horse breeds, some cattle breeds are very similar. Some are more docile in nature and easier to work than others. In versatility competition, the cattle you work might be a mix of everything, purebred or crossbred. The more you work cattle, and watch other people work in versatility, cow-horse and cutting events, the quicker you learn about different breeds of cattle.

Granted, the cow you draw might not be like everybody else's cow that day, but when a pen of cattle comes from the same outfit, the cattle probably have been handled alike and have a similar attitude or mentality. Study the cattle and use that to your advantage.

- Black Angus cattle, originally a British breed, generally are docile and can be good to handle and work. Now, with so many black-cattle crosses, you can't assume all of them are docile; some can be fiery when you put pressure on them.

Although this Charolais-cross has the breed's typical pink nose, not all do.

- Black Limousin cattle, originally bred in France, can be mistaken for Black Angus, but are more "feely" than Angus cattle and can respond quicker. If there's a choice between a Limousin and a Brahma, you might want the Brahma. The Limousin might seem quiet, but can explode. With the Brahma, you know what you're getting to work. Limousin muscling usually is bulky, which makes the Limousin kind of like the halter horse of the cow world.

- Brahma cattle tend to be a little hotter, flightier and quicker than other cattle, but probably are smarter than most. That doesn't necessarily mean Brahma cattle are all bad or flighty; they're just more responsive and react quickly to pressure. Because they're smart, Brahmas figure out how to do things the way they want to do them, rather than the way you do. It takes forethought to handle Brahma cattle, and you must be cautious and precise because there is a fine line between being too far ahead of these cattle and too far behind them.

- Charolais cattle are creamy white with pink noses and pink inside the ears. However, now a lot of Charolais-looking cattle you see actually are first crosses to a Black Angus. The cross' coat is still creamy, but the nose and inside the

Black Angus generally work easier than some of the similar-looking black cross-bred cattle.

ears are black. A smoky-colored cow probably means a Charolais has been crossed three times on a black cow. Charolais characteristics might be in those cattle somewhat, but a lot have been bred out of them. Charolais-cross cattle can be among the favorites to cut from a herd, but, again, each cow you work is so much an individual.

- Herefords, originally a British breed, are red, white-faced cattle. Usually a Hereford cow is considered docile and generally isn't much trouble to handle.

- Longhorn-cross cattle usually are very flighty cattle. Like a Brahma cow, a Longhorn-cross is hotter-natured than a cow of British breeding, such as a Hereford or Angus.

- Salers can be tough cattle to work. They're flighty like the Brahmas, but a little stronger because they don't yield as quickly as Brahmas do. Sometimes it's hard to tell if a cow is a Saler. Most are big, red cattle, but now many are black. They might have a little bit of gray in their tails, and their hair is a little long and curly.

- Simbrah cattle are a Simmental-Brahma cross with characteristics from each breed, the quieter Simmental and the hotter Brahma. But how a Simbrah cow—or any cow—works always comes down to the individual.

A Brangus is a cross between the more docile Angus and the hotter Brahma.

A Simmental-cross is a little more fun to work than a purebred, which plays out quickly.

- Simmental purebred cattle aren't much fun to work because they're like big Holsteins. A Simmental might have a lot of action at first, but doesn't stay that way long at all and quits really quickly.

Settling the Herd

You can learn something about the versatility cattle when riders settle the herd before the ranch cutting starts. Study the cattle to get an indication of which ones might be bad, or good, to work. In versatility competition, the same cattle you work in ranch cutting usually are used for the cow-horse part of the class, so you benefit then, too.

Settling the herd is an art. People ride through the herd until the cattle quit scattering and start to become more docile and used to having a horse come close. Then competitors can ride into the herd without the cattle being intimidated and trying to scatter.

- When you hear that cattle are fresh, it means they haven't been worked in a herd in the cutting or roping pen. Settling these cattle is important because they haven't been handled much. They don't yet understand the horse, so fresh cattle

Watch the herd being settled to get an idea which cattle might be easy to work and which ones are flighty.

might try you hard because they're a little naïve in thinking they can get past your horse.

- When the herd is being settled, watch for individuals in the herd. This cow always throws its head when a rider comes near, or that cow tries to hide behind another one. Usually the cattle are numbered, so pick out those you think might be flighty or "hiders."

- A flighty cow might run back and forth across the pen without giving you an opportunity to show what your horse can do. On the other hand, if you can control a flighty cow and your horse is really good, you probably can score more points than you can on a quiet one. But sometimes a flighty cow lies to you and runs out of energy after only a few seconds of work.

- A hider always tries to stay on the far side of another cow, away from your horse, and often keeps its head down. That hider doesn't want to see you; it's afraid you might attack. Anytime a hider is alone, it panics a little and tries to get back to the herd for security. That makes a hider tough to work. When you finally do work a hider to the front of the herd, you often still must separate the hider from its buddy.

In and Out of the Herd

When you enter the herd in ranch cutting competition, you decide some things, and the cattle decide others. Some things you simply leave up to your turn-back men.

- Always watch for your cow when you ride into the herd. Don't worry about the other cattle. It's the turn-back men's job to take care of them

- When you walk your horse into the herd to bring out your cow to work, it's your choice whether you go into the herd on the left or right side. Do whatever you're most comfortable doing.

- When you spot your designated cow, be very deliberate as you bring it out of the herd to the middle of the arena. Also be very attentive to that cow's head and eye, not its side or its back.

- Realize that flight zones vary with different cattle and affect where you position your horse to control a particular cow. When you start your cow out of the herd, the cow tells you where its flight zone is.

- If a cow's flight zone is far away, realize that you must work the cow on a broad range. Realize, too, that you still can get in that cow's eye and control it from 50 feet away, even though your horse might have to cover four times the distance to get the cow to the middle of the pen and work it there.

- If you come into the right side of the herd, for example, the cattle usually veer a little to the left. Step up and over to keep your cow from going left and head it toward the middle instead.

- Don't push your cow hard when it's with the bunch. Just watch your cow's head and be in position to stop or turn the cow to control the cow's direction. You don't drive your cow out of the herd so much as you block your cow's path back to the herd. Then the only place your cow can go is the middle of the pen, right where you want it.

- If you try to scoop your cow off the front of the herd, most likely that only drives your cow toward the back of the pen. Then you must move toward the back of the herd, too.

- If you must go to the back of the herd, stop your horse for just a second to let the cattle get a little used to you. If you keep moving, they get nervous and want to scatter.

- When your cow is at the front of the herd, try to walk your horse calmly through the herd to your cow. Show the judge that your horse is quiet in the herd and doesn't disturb them. Then make a really good cut to bring out your cow.

- When you make a really pretty cut, a judge might plus your score a point or two. You might not even be close on your cow, but every time it turns, you're there making the right move.

You don't drive a cow out of the herd so much as you block the cow's path to keep it from going back to the herd.

- If you push your cow to the middle of the pen but three or four head come with it, be in position to make your cow stop and stand. Then let the other cattle come back by you.

- With several head in the middle of the pen, you might even have to draw back a bit to keep from putting too much pressure on your cow, but still be in position to stop it until the other cattle are gone. While the turn-backs take care of those three or four head, if your cow tries to move, don't push. Simply step your horse in front of the cow and stop it. Push too much, and you wind up chasing your cow.

- When you stop your cow; you don't turn the cow back. You must have your cow's eye to block it, and you virtually block its view by keeping your horse between the cow and the herd, where it wants to go.

- When the other cattle are cleared from the middle, start your work if you and your cow are far enough in front of the herd. If not, drive your cow a little farther from the herd and stop it again.

- The only time you push your cow hard when coming out of the herd is when your cow is by itself. That's when you drive your cow.

- The greener you and/or your horse, the farther your horse needs to be from a herd, to give you more room to stop the cow. The herd probably takes in 15 to 20 feet from the back of the pen. Your horse should be out from the herd, about another 20 to 30 feet, with your cow on the other side of your horse.

Work Your Cow

Set up your horse to make a good work. Don't get in a hurry in the middle of the pen. Wait until the other cattle have moved away, and then let your turn-back men start moving your cow for you. That's their job. Your job is to stop your cow. That's how you set up your working situation in the ranch cutting.

- When you start working your cow, everything comes down to how much you trust your horse. Do you know he can step up, stop that cow and then come back through the turn quickly enough to do the job?

- If you hurry to move your cow, instead of letting your turn-backs do that, you must push the cow from behind. Then your cow runs from fence to fence or circles around and beats your horse back to the herd.

- No matter how quietly you try to handle cattle, it takes less work to make some cows hot and nervous than it takes for others. A really hot cow can run right through you and your horse trying to get back to its buddies.

- If hurrying to bring the cow out of the herd is the first mistake a novice makes, the second happens when the work starts and a novices pushes his cow too much. When you push your cow too much, your work is more like boxing a cow for the ranch-horse class, rather than cutting.

- Cutting a cow isn't the same as boxing one. In cutting, you stop the cow and let the turn-back men move your cow. You try to set up your cow in a 30- to 40-foot span right in the middle of the arena and work him within that area. When the cow stops and turns, your horse stops, draws back, and then gets in stop position on the cow again. The cow dictates your movement, and you react. Wait for the turn-backs to move your cow. When you box cattle in the working ranch-horse class, you control the cow and show the judge that you can drive that cow wherever you want, then stop and turn it.

- After you cut out your cow, the cow might look at you and break and run, for example, to the left side. Don't push the cow or fall back from it. Work your horse in a straight line across the pen, parallel to the back fence. That's the ideal although sometimes you might have to give a little ground to get back in front of your cow.

- At all times be in position to stop your cow. Many people have a hard time riding to the stop position because their

During the ranch cutting, your horse stops the cow, draws back, turns and moves right back into the stop position on the cow again and again.

horses don't handle well, and they know they'll lose the cow. That's why the training and dry work are important.

- For your horse to learn to handle the cow work, you must understand that everything is based on the stop. Cross the pen and stop the cow. Your turn-back men make the cow move so you can cross the pen again and again and stop the cow again and again.

- When a cow wants to work your horse, that cow might "hit" you five or six times, and you can really show your horse. Take those first good passes a cow gives you and then get your second cow; the first one is about through playing and serious about getting back to the herd.

- Cattle are smarter than you think. When a cow is through playing, it lets you know. It might turn tail and try your turn-back men or run straight at you, then duck and go the other way.

- At a show you must stay in control of your cow at all times. The biggest mistakes are losing control of your cow and not having enough control of your horse to put your cow where you want the cow to be.

Showmanship and Ranch Cutting

One cow you draw in cutting might be a little dead to handle, and another might be high-headed. A third might be a sleeper and seem docile until it's alone in the middle of the pen. When you can control your horse, you can adjust to fit your cow's flight zone and score points with a judge.

- Part of cutting showmanship is being very meticulous in your cuts, which a lot of people don't realize. You can score as much in the herd as you do out front working your cow. When you sort your cow from the herd, watch its eye or head and take control. That doesn't mean you go 90 miles an hour; a slow walk is fine. Try not to disturb the herd.

It takes time and experience to develop enough confidence to rely on your horse to work effectively on a slack rein.

- A judge really likes it when your horse stops and backs through the turn with a cow. Your horse scores up when he works on his back end, and the showmanship is there when you've done your homework.

- Don't try to overshow your horse on the cattle you draw in the cutting pen. When a cow hooks on to work for you, don't stay too long. Once a cow tries the turn-back men, the cow can be twice as hard to hold and determined to get back to the herd. You could lose the cow and points, too. Don't set yourself up for failure.

- With a responsive horse, you probably can score more points with a high-headed, flighty cow. The degree of difficulty is greater, and a judge adds points for that. But your horse must control that type cow in the middle of the pen. Stopping a flighty cow isn't the deal—it's beating the cow back to a herd on the other side after the turn. In this case, hang back a little to give your horse plenty of room to work back and forth across the pen. You can get closer and put more pressure on a quiet cow than you can a flighty one.

A horse that has learned to travel in a collected frame in his dry work is equally eye-appealing when he trots across the pen in his cow work.

- There are markers on the backside of the cutting pen. Anytime your cow comes within 3 feet of a marker, you get a 3-point penalty. That isn't just one time, but every time your cow is at the back fence marker.

- Some people try to work a cow off to the side, instead of in the center of the pen, because it's easy to do and the cow doesn't have much room to run. But with those 3-point penalties, a cow near those markers can be like a pinball machine—ding, ding, ding—and you don't gain a thing in your score.

- Losing a cow back to the herd is a 5-point penalty, but you still can get a score. With five classes in the versatility, you don't know where or when somebody else might mess up, so never quit showing your horse in the cutting—even when you lose a cow. The competition isn't over until all the scores are totaled.

The "Walk-Cow"

I have what I call a "walk-cow" that is really good for cutting practice, especially when it's hard to find cattle to work. The walk-cow is easy to make and easy to use, and I can haul it to a show.

My walk-cow is about the size of a cow, a rectangle 2 ½ feet wide and 7 feet long. It's made from lightweight, 1-inch PVC pipe and has a flag tied in the middle on one end that's used as the head of the cow. I get somebody to stand inside the walk-cow, hold it on either side, and move it back and forth while I work my horse.

The walk-cow works better than a typical "flag" going across the arena because that goes only in a straight line when it reverses direction. Plus, my helper can bring the walk-cow to my horse or draw back, and the 7-foot size is more like a cow, which really helps draw my horse into the turns.

An important thing: My helper shouldn't look at my horse when we work the walk-cow. Otherwise, my horse might start reading my helper instead of the flag at the end of the walk-cow.

The walk-cow is a good training tool when practice cattle aren't readily available.

Control, speed, cow sense, reining and roping—this class has it all.

16

WORKING RANCH-HORSE COMPETITION

The versatility working ranch-horse class demonstrates everything a ranch cowboy wants in his horse—reining ability, cow sense and roping ability. Each competitor works alone in the arena to show how well his horse can perform in those three areas within a 6-minute time limit.

A competitor first runs a reining pattern selected by the judge and posted beforehand. The required maneuvers and scoring are similar to those used in any reining class.

After the reining pattern, the rider calls for his cow to be turned into the arena and first boxes the animal, or holds it at one end of the arena, to demonstrate his horse's control of the cow. Then the rider fences his cow, taking it down the long side of the pen, and turning the cow back along the fence line at least one time in each direction.

Finally, the contestant must rope the cow and bring it to a stop. His horse is judged on his ability to track, rate and stop the cow.

The working ranch-horse class draws attention to the versatility because the cowboy and his work—cattle, riding and roping—still intrigue people. They want to test themselves and their horses with those same challenges.

The Performance Goal

The dry work in this versatility class demonstrates your complete control of your horse. Few people ever experience a great ride on a horse that's right between the reins, so attuned and responsive at any speed. It's all there in that 1,100- or 1,200-pound horse right under you. That power comes from a living animal, and that you have control of him

When a horse is supple and responsive in his dry work, he should be maneuverable enough to fence a cow.

makes the experience unique. How well you manage and direct that power is reflected in your reining score.

In the cow work you continue to control all your horse's power and responsiveness, only in more practical applications. You show the judge that you and your horse can communicate and control a loose cow and then handle it at the end of a rope. You make the most of your control and your horse's power to do the boxing, fencing and roping. When you and your horse can accomplish these things, you make the most of your horsemanship experience. You're partners.

Review Your Skills

The versatility working ranch-horse class, with its flat work, cow work and roping, demands a lot of both you and your horse. But you can meet the challenge when you do your homework. Those same basic maneuvers that serve you well in cutting competition also can carry you through the ranch-horse class cattle work.

That's the big payoff for routinely riding through those flexion, softness and body-control exercises in your warm-ups. You really can't add much to your horse's skills after you get to a show, but when you're there, you sure can take advantage of all the training you have put on your horse at home.

Remember: The basics don't change when you switch from cutting to roping to reining or to any other event. All that changes is how you might combine or use those basics to build a more advanced maneuver, no matter if it's a flying lead change, tracking a cow or turning one on the fence.

Reining Patterns

The reining pattern goes quickly, and getting the pattern correct is crucial. When the pattern is posted at a show, I look over it and go through it in my mind. Then I usually go to the end of the arena to locate the markers and go through the pattern again. I really think about the pattern in terms of the particular horse I'm riding that day.

- If you have trouble remembering the reining pattern, walk through it afoot or draw it on paper. Pay attention to the markers shown on the pattern diagram. Go through the pattern enough times that you know which maneuver comes next and where it should be done.

Dry work in a versatility ranch-horse reining pattern demonstrates how well a horse responds to his rider's control.

- Once you're familiar with the pattern, think about your horse going through the pattern. Which maneuvers can he perform really well? Is there a maneuver that you must really be sharp to help him perform?

- At home, practice performing different reining maneuvers in relation to markers, like you would do each maneuver at a show. Run circles within two cones, change leads at a certain place, or run past a cone to stop.

- Practice reining maneuvers, not patterns, at home. A horse can pick up on a pattern quicker than you can and can anticipate every move you ask him to make.

- Read the rules so that you know which faults give you point deductions, and what can get you disqualified altogether. For example, using equipment the show association terms illegal is a disqualification, but some faults result in a half-point or more being deducted from your score, or possibly a 0 score.

- Although pattern 2, described below, has no cones, other patterns do. When a pattern requires markers, you must be aware of them, but you don't have to look at the markers all the time.

- It can be hard to run the length of the arena and go past an end cone that's almost at the end of the pen. If there's not much space to stop a horse, the judge should notice and reset the marker or cone, but after the first horse has run in competition, a marker can't be changed.

A Tour of Pattern 2

Refer to the diagram shown here for the American Quarter Horse Association's pattern 2 for the working ranch horse class as you read through the pattern maneuvers and tips that follow.

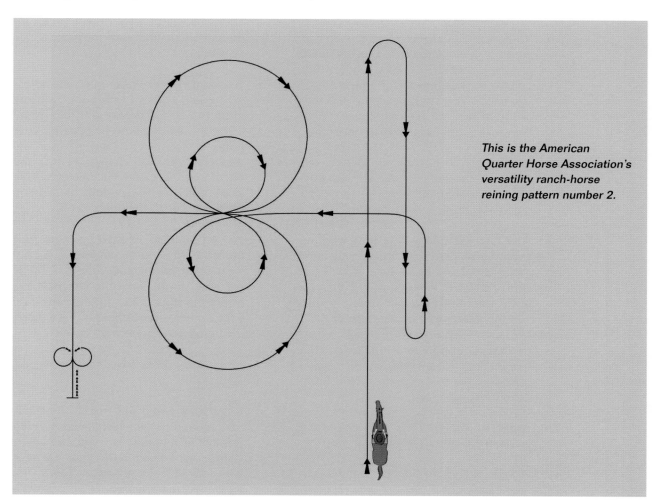

This is the American Quarter Horse Association's versatility ranch-horse reining pattern number 2.

1. Start on the right side of the arena and lope to the far end of the arena.

    • Since you lope down the right side of the arena, your horse should be in the left lead, and you should be at least 20 feet from the fence.

    • About a fourth of the way down the pen, start gaining speed. Keep your horse gathered and flexed at the poll and gain speed gradually.

2. Stop and rollback to right. Continue to the other end of the arena.

    • Continue to gain speed all the way to your stop, to keep it smooth.

    • No cones are shown in the diagram, and there's nothing in the rulebook print about running past a cone before you stop and make your rollback. So pick your place to stop, where the ground seems best.

    • When you build speed into the stop and your horse is gathered and soft in hand, his back end drives deep underneath him, so he goes into the ground easily. If you back off on your speed, the stop isn't pretty. When you let your horse's back flatten, he stops hard on his front end.

    • Don't run your horse completely to the fence on the far end before you stop. You don't want the judge to think the fence is what stops your horse.

    • Any hesitation anywhere in a working ranch-horse pattern is listed, and most patterns tell you to hesitate after a full stop. Pattern 2 doesn't. However, you might want to wait a half-second before you cue your horse for the rollback.

    • Cue with your left foot a little toward the rear on your horse's side, and then, when he leaves the rollback, he should be in the correct right lead.

    • Again, as you go to the other end of the arena, build speed for a smooth stop.

3. Stop and rollback to the left. Continue to the center of the arena.

    • In your rundown, keep your horse gathered, so your stop is smooth and easy. When his body position is correct, he goes softly into the ground.

    • Using your right leg cue, make a smooth rollback to the left and, especially here, be sure your horse is in the correct, left lead as you leave the rollback. That correct lead is important to set up your circles to the left.

    • If your horse takes the incorrect lead leaving the rollback, most judges don't penalize you as long as you change to the correct left lead on the straightaway before you start the next maneuver, a left-hand circle.

4. Lope a small, slow circle to the left. Change leads (to lope on the right lead).

    • If you want to show your horse and your control, and can do this, go into the left-hand circle a bit faster than a slow lope. Then you can rate your horse back into the slow circle and show the judge a nice transition.

    • As you make the circle and come across the middle, think of your circle as being more like a "D" across that line in the center of the arena, to help set up your horse for the lead change. Make the transition, the lead change, right in the middle of the eights, or connected Ds, dead-center in the middle of the pen from one side to the other.

    • As you come across the D, pick up your horse's right shoulder and move his hip right for a pretty lead change. Usually the slower you lope, the tougher it is to get the change, but the more you do your homework on the basic dry work, the better your horse performs.

5. Lope a right circle with medium speed. Change leads.

    • Rate your speed and make the circle really round on the outside and then flat through the middle, so you can easily change leads again. To do that, you must look ahead, where you're going, not down at the ground or at your horse's shoulder. When you look down, you're not on target at the center and usually are late with your lead-change cues.

- The main thing: Show a difference in the size and the speed of your circles. You can plus some points when you show those variations.

6. Lope a large fast circle to the left. Change leads (to lope on the right lead).

- Initially, all that changes here is the size and speed of your circle.

- The basic maneuvers you use to change from the left to the right lead remain the same. Think and ride step-by-step to help your horse change leads cleanly.

7. Lope a large fast circle to the right. Change leads (to the left lead).

- Remember that you've simply changed direction to go the other way on your other lead.

- Both the size and speed of the circle remain the same. Try your best to keep this large right circle approximately the same size as the large left-hand circle you have just ridden.

- Follow the same steps as you move your horse's shoulders and hips to switch from the right to the left lead.

8. Continue down the arena.

- Your horse should be in the left lead for the final rundown of the pattern.

- Again, look up and ahead, and gain speed as you ride toward the stop.

9. Stop and back 10 to 15 feet.

- Be sure your horse is gathered and soft in hand before you ask him to stop. If he isn't, elevate your reins slightly and use your legs to drive him forward into the bit. He should round his back and flex at the poll so you can have an easy stop.

- When your horse really backs smoothly and quickly, it's a plus to the judge.

My Cheat-Sheet Thumb

Even though I'm familiar with the ranch-horse reining patterns, there are times in the arena when I thinking about something else and can't remember exactly what I need to do next. Anybody can forget something in a reining pattern.

Before I show in the dry work, I write the pattern maneuvers on my thumb. In pattern 2, I know the first maneuver is a rundown. The rollback is to the right, so I write an "R" on my thumb, and I know the next rollback is to the left. With the first circle marked "L," I know I have to change leads and then circle to the right.

In the arena, I might be thinking more of the maneuver than its direction, so I make a mark for each maneuver on my thumb, just to keep me on track in the pattern.

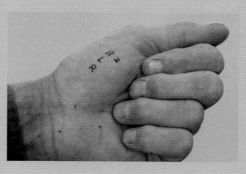

- In the back, your horse shouldn't push against the bridle with his mouth gapped. If necessary, use your feet to drive your horse off the bridle so he's soft in the poll. Then smooch and ask him to back.

10. Do a 360-degree spin right or left.

11. Do a 360-degree spin opposite direction taken in step 10.

- With only two spins in pattern 2, one in each direction, speed isn't such an issue since you don't have much opportunity to show what your horse can do.

- Be sure each of the two spins is correct. When you make only one spin each way, let your horse take his first crossover step or two slowly, and then pick up speed if he can keep his footwork correct.

- In other patterns requiring two spins in each direction, use the first half of the first spin to be correct. Then add speed to the remaining one and a half spins each way to complete the maneuver.

12. Hesitate to show completion of pattern.

- That slight hesitation gives you a moment to acknowledge the judge.

- The hesitation also lets the judge know you're through showing your horse and that your horse can stand quietly.

Reining Showmanship

- Know where the cones or markers are in the reining pattern and be sure to read the print for the pattern. The print explains what you think you're looking at in the ranch-horse patterns.

- It's hard to ask everything of a horse every time you ride into the show pen, and sometimes you might not have to do

Gauge the arena dirt before you ask your horse to stop hard and slide. Don't ask him for more than the dirt will allow.

that. You gain or lose versatility points in many ways in several classes. Try to keep track of your points so you know if you must really ask a lot of your horse for a great reining score, or if you have the point room to just make a solid run.

- If the ground at a show isn't good for stopping and sliding, don't ask your horse to stop hard and try to slide. You can cripple him. Gauge the dirt as best you can.

- When you must stop at, not past, a marker, you can start your stop right at the marker and slide past it. But if you start the stop before you get to the marker, even though you do slide past it, the judge can dock you for stopping before you reach the cone.

- Realize what all good hands know. After you train your horse, you spend the rest of your life trying to keep him from anticipating the next move. Your horse must learn to wait and listen for you to tell him what to do—not beat you to the cue for the next maneuver.

Box Your Cow

First, remember the difference between cutting a cow and boxing one. In cutting, the turn-back men move your cow, and you keep it in the middle of the pen. Your horse stops, draws back and then moves over to stop the cow again and again, but the cow dictates your movement.

When you box a cow, you control it and drive it across the pen with more leeway as you go from side to side. When the cow stops, step up and move the cow back across the pen. You dictate the cow's movement.

- At a show, the same cattle used for the cutting often are used for the working ranch-horse class. The cow you draw might not be so good for one class, but could work well for you in the other.

- If you're not familiar with the cattle, make sure you're some distance away from the gate when you call for your cow in the ranch-horse class. Be 30 or even 40 feet past the center marker that's usually in the arena before you call for the cow.

When boxing a cow, you dictate when the cow moves across the pen; there's no turn-back rider to do that for you as there is in ranch cutting.

- Sometimes the facilities aren't set up too well to have one cow cut off from the herd, and that cow can be disturbed and come out running. The cow usually is watching the people who drive it out of the pen and doesn't always look up and see you at first. If you're too close to the gate, the cow could blow by you and run to the backside of the arena.

- Even when your cow is flighty coming into the arena, and you have to stay way back, you still must establish eye contact and hold that cow. No matter which direction the cow breaks, get over there and stop it. Don't push the cow yet; just hold it there.

- If your cow is really rank, you might even have to give ground, but a judge doesn't discredit you at all if you're always in the right position on the cow. Fall a horse-length behind your cow, and the judge deducts 1 point.

- When your cow comes into the arena, you must stop the cow and take control. The cow might try you and your horse three, four or five times before it stops. Then you usually can turn and go to the other end with your cow. When you do, just follow and try to keep your cow moving to the end of the arena; then start your boxing.

- In another scenario, you might draw a quiet cow that can work your horse, but is respectful of him. When that cow comes out the gate into the arena, it's still a good idea not to be too close. Like you do with the flighty cow, get in that quiet cow's eye and gain control before you push it to the end and start boxing.

- To box your cow at the end of the pen, first stop it. Then step up to the cow and drive it across the pen to the other side, where you again stop it and turn it back across the pen. Show the judge how well you and your horse can control the cow as you move it back and forth across the pen, stop and turn it.

- When you drive your cow, your position is at its rib cage or hip, but as you go past the cow to stop and turn with it, make sure your horse stops and comes right back, too. Your horse is in contact with the cow at all times.

- Don't take your cow completely from one arena fence to the other. Try to stay 15 or 20 feet from the arena side fence to show your control, but that isn't always possible.

- Even if you can set up the cow to work your horse a little bit, you still must stop the cow. Then you can step your horse back from the cow, turn and drive it across the pen.

- When boxing, you also try to take a little air out of your cow and get that cow to respect your horse. Doing that helps develop the control you need for the fencing part of the competition. When you think you've boxed your cow enough to do that, take the cow down the fence.

Fence Your Cow

When you've suppled and flexed your horse in the dry work, your horse should be able to fence a cow easily. With a soft face, spine and rib cage, he can make those big stops and come back pretty with the cow, and it's an easy ride for you.

- When you take your cow down the fence, stay at the cow's hip to keep it against the fence.

- How close your horse is to the cow depends on how fast the cow is and/ or how big the show is. To place in the versatility at a big show, you might want to get tight on the cow and add a little pressure to make something happen to show what your horse can do. The closer you are, the faster the cow will go.

- Don't come out of your boxing and let your cow hang up in the corner of the pen. That puts you at a disadvantage.

When you try to push your cow out of the corner, it could come off the fence to get a jump on you going down the fence.

- Drive your cow down the fence until you pass the center marker before you make your move. Otherwise, there's a 1-point penalty. After the center marker, ride your horse up and even with the cow, and then get into position to stop your cow and turn your cow along the fence. Don't blow by the cow. Just move your horse up and into the stop position.

- When you're even with the cow, if the cow honors your horse and stops, that's great. If your cow doesn't honor your horse and stop, let your horse take that 5 or 6 inches on the cow. Then, when the cow comes back in the turn, your horse can stay with it.

- If you must go 6 inches past the cow to stop it, your horse has the opportunity to come back through the turn and stay hooked up with your cow. When you go beyond those 6 inches, you overshoot your opportunity to control your cow.

- When a cow doesn't make that stop, step up your horse slowly. If you step up too fast and drive your horse by the cow, the cow stops, but it also takes longer for your horse to stop and turn because he's going faster and is farther past the cow. That's a messy turn, and the cow could duck behind your horse.

- In the turn, if the cow ducks behind your horse and heads to the middle of the pen, it's best to circle the cow around the other way. It seldom works if you try to drive the cow right back to the fence instead of circling, and it's never pretty There are no deductions for circling a cow although somebody who keeps his animal on the fence outscores you.

- Everybody thinks fencing is a horse race. It isn't. Instead of driving hard past the cow, let your horse ease by the cow. That makes everything go slowly and gives you control of the cow in the turn.

- Most people also think going down the fence is scary, and speed scares them.

When a cow moves at 20 miles an hour, you need to go only slightly faster to fence the cow, not 5 or 10 miles an hour faster than the cow.

Think of it this way: If your cow goes 20 miles an hour, you don't need to go 25 to 30. You can go only 21 miles per hour or so and barely ease by the cow. Take that approach, and you slow down the comeback on the fence a lot.

• The problem with speed is a lack of control. Control always goes back to the downward transitions, and speed comes back to teaching your horse how to run, both discussed previously in the book. Build your horse's speed and your control at home.

• If speed bothers you or your horse, the best thing to do is go roping. Drive your horse to the cow's hip, rope and stop your horse. That helps you get comfortable with the speed and maintain control, and your horse, too.

- If you can, turn your cow into the fence. Then your cow has to make the same moves your horse does. If the cow turns toward the center of the pen, there's hardly any way your horse can turn and beat the cow to take him down the fence again. Instead, you have to circle the cow and then bring him back to the fence.

- When you're good at controlling your cow and can drive the cow's head into the turn toward the fence, the judge pluses your turns almost every time.

- When you make the turn on the fence, don't ever quit riding your horse. That one common mistake lets the cow take control. Keep riding until you have your horse right back in position to take that cow down the fence the other way. When you quit riding, you lose control.

- Don't allow your horse to "kind of" stop and "sort of" turn when he fences cattle because he gets front-endy. He's not working off his hindquarters or soft in the face. He's rough to ride and might cripple himself.

- In the versatility ranch-horse, make the two turns on the fence, one in each direction, and then rope your cow. In a reined or working cow-horse class, people fence the cow three or four times, mostly to take air out of the cow so the rider can circle the cow both ways. In versatility you can fence all you want, but a judge doesn't plus you points for three turns, and he minuses your score if you mess up one of the turns.

- If your cow is still flighty after you've boxed and fenced it, get ready to rope and track the cow around the pen to tire it. There's no deduction for tracking, but could be a deduction if you mess up extra turns fencing.

Rope Your Cow

By the time you're ready to build your loop, you're usually in a trot because the cow

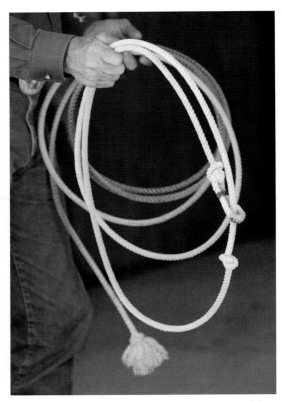

A knot-rope can help a horse learn how to hold a cow and is convenient for use at home on practice cattle.

is a little winded by then. The cow probably has come off the fence, too, looking for its buddies. Don't stop your horse to build your loop. Build it while you trot behind the cow. That shows you're still in the game, controlling the shots—not fretting, stopping and starting again. Stay in control of your cow even when you build your loop.

- When you want to get your rope, don't let your horse's forward motion die. Keep moving across the pen and try to stay with the cow a little bit to show your control. You don't have to stay right on top of the cow, but keep a good trot until you get your loop built.

- As you build your loop, set up your cow for roping. Bring your cow around for that right-hand turn you want. You don't want your cow to go to the corner and stay there. Pressure the cow to go down the fence so you can ride into position behind the cow and rope.

- As for tracking when you rope in the working ranch-horse part of the

When a horse holds position on a cow, as Whiskey did at the American Quarter Horse Association versatility ranch-horse finals in Denver, anything is possible, even a world title.

Black Hope Stik, a daughter of Smart Whiskey Doc, was instrumental in earning the inaugural 2010 Project Cowboy title. The mare performed not only bridleless reining maneuvers, but also bridleless cattle work—boxing, fencing, circling and roping—and received a standing ovation from appreciative spectators.

WORKING RANCH-HORSE COMPETITION

WORKING RANCH-HORSE COMPETITION

versatility, a judge pluses your score when your horse runs up and into position to track the cow, then rates off by himself and stays in that position.

- A judge also likes to see that you don't really have to pick up the reins to move your horse to the right when the cow heads right. Your horse is locked onto that cow, and your reins are slack so you can concentrate on roping.

- You might rope when you circle your cow to set it up to go down the fence. If you don't, and you take the fence to the left, and you're a right-handed roper, that cow gets against the fence, and you can't rope it. Remember to position your cow where you have the best opportunity to throw your loop and make a good catch.

- In another scenario, your cow might come across the end of the pen, going to the right, and you should be on the cow's right hip at that point to control the cow. As you first come out of the corner to go down the fence, step your horse in behind the cow. Line up your right knee roughly with the cow's back, but not as far to the left as you might have it when you team rope. Even though your horse might cover the cow a little, it's so easy to stand up in the stirrups and rope.

- Don't try to rope a cow headed toward where the herd is penned because that cow usually runs hard to get to its buddies. Too, if you don't rope that cow before it gets headed back to the herd, you could crash the cow into the fence, and that's not being a good cowboy. Instead, drive the cow past the herd and then rope when the cow is reluctant to leave the herd and can be rated.

- When you rope, you must make a legal neck catch, so know the rules for the show you enter. Some bad catches leave you with a no-score. With other bad catches, if you're cowboy enough to grab your rope and pull it off the cow, you can rebuild your loop and keep going.

- After you catch the cow, sit deep in your saddle and say whoa to your horse. The judge wants to see if your horse really gets into the ground when he stops and how soft and easy he makes the stop.

- You lose points for your first miss, but remember that this class is one-fifth of your total score, with roping only a portion of that fifth.

- In some versatility classes, you must pull the cow at least 10 feet, but in AQHA shows, all you do is stop the cow and turn it to face you.

- The biggest problem in all the cattle classes is that when people go fast, their horses are out of control. If you've never ridden your horse very fast and worked with him, you can't expect that control. Practice and learn to control your horse with speed, and you'll be so surprised at how much better things can be. When you're comfortable running up to rope a cow and can stop your horse, you realize that you can run up beside a cow going down the fence, and it's no big deal.

- Breakaway roping at home is good practice, but your horse never feels the jerk like he does when you stop a cow. At a show, where your horse has to take that jerk, it can pull him out of the ground.

- At home, use a knot-rope so that your horse gets the jerk and learns how to hold the cow without coming out of the ground. A knot in the rope keeps it from drawing completely tight around a cow's neck. When you rope, your horse feels the jerk when you catch, and when the cow faces him, the rope comes off its head easily.

- When you practice roping at home, if you miss, bring your horse back to you in a downward transition, and let the cow go. You might ride your horse in a little circle and then take him back to the cow.

- At home don't let your horse get pushy going to a cow. Bring your horse back to you. You might even stop, if you must, and then lope him again. Don't make a big issue of this; just do it.

REVIEW YOUR SKILLS

- Remember: How your horse handles on the ground reflects how he'll ride when you're in the saddle. (See Chapter 5.)

- When you ride, get the edge off your horse first, before you start training or introducing anything new. (See Chapter 6.)

- When your horse seems relaxed and willing to listen, check his lateral flexion. Is he soft and supple? (See Chapter 6.)

- Ask your horse to soften his poll and frame his body from head to tail. If necessary, use the pull-to-the-hip exercise to lighten his response. (See Chapter 6.)

- Move your horse's forehand—on and off the arc of a circle, in a figure eight, and in the serpentine. Counterbend him in a figure eight and back him through one, too, and flex, or "hinge," his nose right and left while loping a circle. (See Chapter 7.)

- Move your horse's hips as you travel down a fence line, in a circle and in a straight line in the open. (See Chapter 7.)

- Move your horse's rib cage to the right and the left. (See Chapter 7.)

- Keep your horse's poll soft and his body in frame and driving off the hindquarters at all gaits—walk, trot, extended trot, lope and extended lope. (See Chapter 8.)

- Be sure that your horse continues to hold his soft frame as he performs basic stops, backs and turns. (See Chapter 8.)

- Side-pass your horse in each direction or work him in the 12-foot box. (See Chapter 9.)

- Back your horse in a circle and perform cutter-style rollbacks in each direction, which prepares him for the cow work. (See Chapter 9).

- Circle your horse in a fast walk for a few rounds, then walk him down in turnarounds in each direction. (See Chapter 9.)

- Check your horse's rate at a trot and a lope. (See Chapter 10.)

- Also check your horse's response to the three stop signals—the word whoa, the lift of your reins and your changing leg position—at a walk, trot and canter. If necessary, pinch down the reins in the stop to lighten his response. (See Chapter 10.)

- Stop your horse, and ask him to back. Use your feet to make your horse move his. Work with him until he backs quickly and easily. (See Chapter 10.)

- Ride your horse in circles and vary the size and speed to check his maneuverability and rate. (See Chapter 11.)

- Ride your horse through the motions for a lead change although it isn't necessary to actually change leads. As you trot and canter, elevate his shoulder and move his hip in each direction. (See Chapter 11.)

- Find a new "obstacle" in the pasture for your horse to approach, or make a new one from whatever is handy—crossties, hay bales, barrels, etc. (See Chapter 12.)

- Practice roping the dummy while you're afoot. (See Chapter 13.)

- Also practice roping the dummy while you're horseback. (See Chapter 13.)

- Track a cow around the pen. You might even practice swinging your rope while you track. (See Chapter 14.)

- Practice the cutter-style rollback as dry-work preparation for working cattle, so your horse understands how to respond. (See Chapter 14.)

- Work a few head of cattle. Put your horse in the stop position, back him into the turn, and give him time to hook onto the cow. (See Chapter 14.)

- Watch cattle being settled at a local cutting or how different cattle react at the local sale barn. (See Chapter 15.)

- Ride in a practice cutting similar to a versatility ranch cutting at a show, complete with turn-backs and herd holders.

- At the practice cutting, take the time to work on your technique as you and your horse enter the herd and work your cow. (See Chapter 15.)

- At a show, walk through the posted reining pattern. Then stand at the end of the arena and mentally place the markers in the pen and again ride through the pattern in your mind. (See Chapter 16.)

- Think about boxing, driving and fencing cattle, rather than cutting, to prepare for the working ranch-horse class. (See Chapter 16.)

- Use a knot-rope at home so your horse learns how to handle the jerk and the cow at a show. (See Chapter 16.)

- Keep versatility competition in perspective. Each maneuver is only a portion of the requirements for each class, and each class represents only a fifth of your total score.

PROFILE: FRAN DEVEREUX SMITH

Fran Devereux Smith joined the *Western Horseman* staff in 1992, initially as a staff writer, and in 1993 became an associate editor with the magazine. She then served as managing editor of the magazine for several years before becoming book publishing director for *Western Horseman*'s book division.

A broad-based background in the equine industry has proven an asset to Fran's work in equine journalism. A lifelong horsewoman, she grew up showing horses and rodeoing, qualifying for the College National Finals Rodeo and representing her home state as Miss Rodeo Arkansas. As an adult, Fran continued showing, primarily reining horses, but competed in everything from hunt-seat classes to team penning, and she has ridden trails nationwide. Fran also spent several years training horses, giving riding instruction and participating in the family cattle work before coming to *Western Horseman*.

Books Published by WESTERN HORSEMAN

BACON & BEANS
by Stella Hughes
144 pages and 200-plus recipes for delicious Western chow.

BARREL RACING
Completely Revised
by Sharon Camarillo
128 pages, 158 photographs and 17 illustrations. Foundation horsemanship and barrel racing skills for horse and rider with additional tips on feeding, hauling and winning.

CHARMAYNE JAMES ON BARREL RACING
by Charmayne James with Cheryl Magoteaux
192 pages and 200-plus color photographs. Training techniques and philosophy from the most successful barrel racer in history. Vignettes that illustrate Charmayne's approach to identifying and correcting barrel-racing problems, as well as examples and experiences from her 20-plus years as a world-class competitor.

COWBOYS & BUCKAROOS
by Tim O'Byrne
176 pages and more than 250 color photograps. From an industry professional, trade secrets and working lifestyle of these North American icons. The cowboy crew's four seasons of the cattle-industry year, buckaroo and cowboy lingo and the Cowboy Code by which they live. How they start colts, handle cattle, make long circles in rough terrain and much, much more, including excerpts from the author's journal.

COW-HORSE CONFIDENCE
By Martin Black with Cynthia McFarland
190 pages, more than 235 vintage and full-color photos and illustrations. This top hand, clinician and competitor explains how thoughtful stockmanship practices can help you develop a responsive cow-working partner and make the experience as low-stress as possible for you, your horse and the cattle you're working.

CUTTING
by Leon Harrel
144 pages and 200 photographs. Complete guide to this popular sport involving cattle and from an award-winning, cutting-horse industry professional.

FIRST HORSE
by Fran Devereux Smith
176 pages, 160 black-and-white photos and numerous illustrations. Step-by-step information for the first-time horse owner and/or novice rider.

HELPFUL HINTS FOR HORSEMEN
128 pages and 325 photographs and illustrations. WH readers' and editors' tips on every facet of life with horses. Solutions to common problems horse owners share. Chapter titles: Equine Health Care; Saddles; Bits and Bridles; Gear; Knots; Trailers/Hauling Horses; Trail Riding/Backcountry Camping; Barn Equipment; Watering Systems; Pasture, Corral and Arena Equipment; Fencing and Gates; Odds and Ends.

IMPRINT TRAINING
by Robert M. Miller, D.V.M.
144 pages and 250 photographs. How to "program" newborn foals.

LEGENDARY RANCHES
By Holly Endersby, Guy de Galard, Kathy McRaine and Tim O'Byrne
240 pages and 240 color photos. Explores the cowboys, horses, history and traditions of contemporary North American ranches. Adams, Babbitt, Bell, Crago, CS, Dragging Y, Four Sixes, Gang, Haythorn, O RO, Pitchfork, Stuart and Waggoner.

LEGENDS 1
by Diane C. Simmons with Pat Close
168 pages and 214 photographs. Barbra B, Bert, Chicaro Bill, Cowboy P-12, Depth Charge (TB), Doc Bar, Go Man Go, Hard Twist, Hollywood Gold, Joe Hancock, Joe Reed P-3, Joe Reed II, King P-234, King Fritz, Leo, Peppy, Plaudit, Poco Bueno, Poco Tivio, Queenie, Quick M Silver, Shue Fly, Star Duster, Three Bars (TB), Top Deck (TB) and Wimpy P-1.

LEGENDS 2
by Jim Goodhue, Frank Holmes, Phil Livingston and Diane C. Simmons
192 pages and 224 photographs. Clabber, Driftwood, Easy Jet, Grey Badger II, Jessie James, Jet Deck, Joe Bailey P-4 (Gonzales), Joe Bailey (Weatherford), King's Pistol, Lena's Bar, Lightning Bar, Lucky Blanton, Midnight, Midnight Jr, Moon Deck, My Texas Dandy, Oklahoma Star, Oklahoma Star Jr., Peter McCue, Rocket Bar (TB), Skipper W, Sugar Bars and Traveler.

LEGENDS 3
by Diane Ciarloni, Jim Goodhue, Kim Guenther, Frank Holmes, Betsy Lynch and Larry Thornton, 208 pages and 196 photographs. Flying Bob, Hollywood Jac 86, Jackstraw (TB), Maddon's Bright

Eyes, Mr Gun Smoke, Old Sorrel, Piggin String (TB), Poco Dell, Poco Lena, Poco Pine, Question Mark, Quo Vadis, Royal King, Showdown, Steel Dust and Two Eyed Jack.

LEGENDS 4
Various Authors
216 pages and 216 photographs. Blondy's Dude, Dash For Cash, Diamonds Sparkle, Doc O'Lena, Ed Echols, Fillinic, Harlan, Impressive, Lady Bug's Moon, Miss Bank, Miss Princess/Woven Web (TB), Rebel Cause, Tonto Bars Hank, Vandy, Zan Parr Bar, Zantanon, Zippo Pine Bar.

LEGENDS 5
by Alan Gold, Sally Harrison,
Frank Holmes and Ty Wyant
248 pages, approximately 300 photographs. Bartender, Bill Cody, Chicado V, Chubby, Custus Rastus (TB), Hank H, Jackie Bee, Jaguar, Joe Cody, Joe Moore, Leo San, Little Joe, Monita, Mr Bar None, Pat Star Jr., Pretty Buck, Skipa Star, and Topsail Cody.

LEGENDS 6
by Patti Campbell, Sally Harrison, Frank Holmes, GloryAnn Kurtz, Cheryl Magoteaux, Heidi Nyland, Bev Pechan and Juli S. Thorson
236 pages, approximately 270 photographs. Billietta, Caseys Charm, Colonel Freckles, Conclusive, Coy's Bonanza, Croton Oil, Doc Quixote, Doc's Prescription, Dynamic Deluxe, Flit Bar, Freckles Playboy, Great Pine, Jewels Leo Bars, Major Bonanza, Mr San Peppy, Okie Leo, Paul A, Peppy San, Speedy Glow and The Invester.

LEGENDS 7
by Frank Holmes, Glory Ann Kurtz, Cheryl Magoteaux, Bev Pechan, Honi Roberts, Heather S. Thomas and Juli Thorson
260 pages and 300-plus photos. Big Step, Boston Mac, Commander King, Cutter Bill, Doc's Dee Bar, Doc's Oak, Gay Bar King, Hollywood Dun It, Jazabell Quixote, Mr Conclusion, Otoe, Peppy San Badger, Quincy Dan, Rey Jay, Rugged Lark, Skip A Barb, Sonny Dee Bar, Te N' Te, Teresa Tivio and War Leo.

NATURAL HORSE-MAN-SHIP
by Pat Parelli
224 pages and 275 photographs. Parelli's six keys to a natural horse-human relationship.

PROBLEM-SOLVING, VOLUME 1
by Marty Marten
248 pages and more than 250 photos and illustrations. How to develop a willing partnership between horse and human and improve hard-to-catch, barn-sour, herd-bound and spooking horses and trailer-loading, water-crossing and pull-back problems.

PROBLEM-SOLVING, VOLUME 2
by Marty Marten
231 page with photos and illustrations. A continuation of Volume 1. How-to training techniques for halter-breaking; hoof- and leg-handling, neck-reining and trail-riding problems; cinchy and head-shy horses. Sound approaches to trail riding and working cattle.

RAISE YOUR HAND IF YOU LOVE HORSES
by Pat Parelli with Kathy Swan
224 pages and 200-plus black-and-white and color photos. Autobiography of the world's foremost proponent of natural horsemanship. Pat Parelli's experiences, from the clinician's earliest remembrances to the opportunities he's enjoyed in the last decade. Bonus anecdotes from Pat's friends.

RANCH HORSEMANSHIP
by Curt Pate with Fran Devereux Smith
220 pages and more than 250 color photos and illustrations. How almost any rider at almost any level of expertise can adapt ranch-horse-training techniques to help his mount become a safer more enjoyable ride. Curt's methods help prepare rider and horse for whatever they might encounter in the round pen, arena, pasture and beyond.

REINING,
Completely Revised
by Al Dunning
216 pages and 300-plus photographs. Complete how-to training for this exciting exciting event from one of the winningest horsemen ever.

RIDE SMART
by Craig Cameron with Kathy Swan
224 pages and more than 250 black-and-white and color photos. Craig Cameron's view of horses as a species and how to develop a positive, partnering relationship with them, along with solid horsemanship skills suited for both novice and experienced riders. Ground-handling techniques, hobble-breaking methods, colt-starting, high-performance maneuvers and trailer-loading. Trouble-shooting tips and personal anecdotes about Craig's life.

RIDE THE JOURNEY
by Chris Cox with Cynthia McFarland
228 pages and 200-plus color photos. Insightful training methods from Chris Cox, 2007 and 2008 The Road to the Horse Champion. Step-by-step techniques for gaining confidence and horsemanship expertise, and for helping your equine partner reach his full potential in the arena, on the ranch or down the trail. From theory to practical application, equine psychology, natural head-set, horsemanship basics, collection and advanced maneuvers. Chapters on trail riding, starting colts and working cattle.

RODEO LEGENDS
by Gavin Ehringer
216 pages and vintage photos and life stories of rodeo greats. Joe Alexander, Jake Barnes, Joe Beaver, Leo Camarillo, Clay O'Brien Cooper, Roy Cooper, Tom Ferguson, Bruce Ford, Marvin Garrett, Don Gay, Tuff Hedeman, Charmayne James, Bill Linderman, Larry Mahan, Ty Murray, Dean Oliver, Jim Shoulders, Casey Tibbs, Harry Tompkins and Fred Whitfield.

STARTING COLTS
by Mike Kevil
168 pages and 400 photographs. Step-by-step procedure for starting colts.

THE HANK WIESCAMP STORY
by Frank Holmes
208 pages and 260-plus photographs. The biography of the legendary breeder of Quarter Horses, Appaloosas and Paints.

TEAM ROPING WITH JAKE AND CLAY
by Fran Devereux Smith
224 pages and more than 200 photographs and illustrations. Solid information for fast times from multiple world champions Jake Barnes and Clay O'Brien Cooper. Rope-handling techniques, roping dummies, and heading and heeling for practice and in competition. Sound advice about rope horses, roping steers, gear and horsemanship.

TRAIL RIDING
by Janine M. Wilder
128 pages and 150-plus color photographs. From a veteran trail rider, a comprehensive guide covering all the bases needed to enjoy this fast-growing sport. Proven methods for developing a solid trail horse, safe ways to handle various terrain, solutions for common trail problems, plus tips and resources for traveling with horses. Interesting sidebars about Janine's experiences on the trail.

UNDERSTANDING LAMENESS
By Terry Swanson, DVM, with Heidi Nyland
207 pages, plus glossary; more than 160 color photographs, plus radiographs and illustrations. Dr. Terry Swanson guides you through various equine lamenesses and how each can affect your horse's future health and serviceability. Swanson considers lameness symptoms and which diagnostic techniques and treatments are best-suited to manage particular problems.

WELL-SHOD
by Don Baskins
160 pages, 300 black-and-white photos and illustrations. A horse-shoeing guide for owners and farriers. Easy-to-read, step-by-step information about how to trim and shoe horses for a variety of uses. Special attention to corrective shoeing for horses with various foot and leg problems.

WIN WITH BOB AVILA
by Juli S. Thorson
Hardbound, 128 full-color pages. World champion Bob Avila's philosophies for succeeding as a competitor, breeder and trainer. The traits that separate horse-world achievers from also-rans.

WORLD CLASS REINING
by Shawn Flarida and Craig Schmersal with Kathy Swan
160 pages and 200-plus color photos. The sources' complete training program that catapulted them to reining stardom. Horse selection, training philosophies, basic foundation principles, exercises and training techniques for reining maneuvers, plus show preparation and competition strategies.

Western Horseman, established in 1936, is the world's leading horse publication.
For subscription information: 800-877-5278.

To order other *Western Horseman* books:
800-874-6774 • *Western Horseman,* 2112 Montgomery St., Fort Worth, TX 76107

Web site: **www.westernhorseman.com.**